HEY, CANCER! IT'S MY Birthday again!

RAFAEL (NUNI) CUEVAS, JR.

NEW VISION
PUBLISHING HOUSE

HEY, CANCER! IT'S MY BIRTHDAY AGAIN

ISBN: 978-0-578-51488-8

New Vision Publishing House

Tampa, Florida

Dedication

I never imagined my life embodied in a book, much less that it would be of inspiration to many. For this reason, I dedicate this project primarily to the author of my life, Jesus Christ. Thank you, Jesus, for being my faithful friend. My sweet companion. My Father. The handkerchief of my many tears. You have never abandoned me. You have always been faithful to Your promises. You have given me life and life in abundance. Your love is eternal. Thank you for choosing me to speak about You. Everything I have and all that I am, I owe it to You. Serving you is my honor and my great privilege. I long for the day when I can finally hug You and kiss Your beautiful face. Regardless of what happens in this life, You and I will always remain friends. Until the day I die, I will live on this earth, giving You all the glory, the honor, and all my thankfulness.

To my wife, Shaina Marie Cuevas. Because none of my dreams seem crazy to you. Everything is possible according to your Faith. Since I met you, most of the things

I have achieved have been because you trust God. I've never met anyone who carries as much Faith as you. Daily, you are my inspiration. So today, I can say that this book exists thanks to God and you. I love you, baby.

Acknowledgements

To my Dad, Pastor Rafael Cuevas Sr.

Thank you for training me for what would be the hardest and most challenging fight of my life. I'm grateful for all the nights where we would pray and fast together. The many hours of Bible study prepared me not only to be the man of God I am today, but also to fight cancer. Daddy, we didn't get into boxing, but we reached the hearts of thousands of people through the message of Jesus. You will always be my hero, and I will always be your "Macho Man."

To my mother, Pastor Lourdes Cuevas.

Thank you for caring for me in that hospital. You never stopped praying so that I could be healed of cancer. Above all, I am grateful to you for giving me the gift of birth. In a world where abortion is favored, you accepted the challenge of giving me life in 1985 and later declared this beautiful calling upon me. Today, for the Glory of God, I am exercising the privilege of being an Evangelist.

To my sisters Yajaira and Fanny.

Fanny, I am so grateful for the way you cared for me at that hospital. Yajaira, thank you for being the first worshiper in my crusades. As children, you were the first to hear my sermons. Thank you for applauding me, even if what I said didn't make sense. I am also grateful to you.

To my Aunt Maria Laboy.

Thank you for always standing at the front row of all my victories. For answering all my calls, even late at night, while I was living in that hospital. For telling me: "There is no pain." For telling me: "You will soon come out of this trial." And most of all, because you were the first to write the title of my book on paper. You are my earth angel; I love you. This book is also yours!

To my first cousin Andrés Cuevas.

Thank you for being my right hand and for dreaming with me. You are the older brother I've always wanted. I also thank you for becoming my life's bodyguard, assuring that I always focus on what God said about me and not on the many tribulations I have faced. The crisis did not last;

however, our love is eternal. I love you, brother of my soul.

To my Aunt and Uncle Laura and Gilberto Cuevas.

Because you were my comforting balm in the most challenging storms of my life. For loving me, not as a nephew, but as a son. Uncle, Auntie, the sun has risen! I love you.

To my niece Yadeliz Divina Pérez de Cuevas.

Because of you, I have the title of uncle. Thank you for visiting me in that hospital. Every time you entered the room, the darkness fled. Remember to always smile, for there is power in your smile. Even the gloomiest room lights up as you smile. I love you.

To my nephews Edgar and Jeremy.

You helped me to believe that I am nothing less than what God says about me. Thank you for loving me when I thought everyone had stopped. Also, for being the first ones to tell me that I am their role model. I love you.

To our international coordinator, Jose Arzola (Father).

Thank you for working with Divine Healing Ministries for the last 14 years. For your Faith, not only in me, but also in this ministry. I don't know why you love me so much, but I thank God that you love me as you do. This victory is also your victory. Love you!

To my dear friend David Ramos.

Thank you for being my brother in times of trouble. You never lost Faith in my miracle. You never left me alone in that hospital. Others abandoned me and forgot about me, but not you! Your visits were a refreshment for my soul. This victory also belongs to you. I love you, brother!

To the prophet Carlos Ramirez Jr. (Carlitos).

Thank you for allowing yourself to be used by God in my childhood so that I could be an evangelist today. I have always admired you and will always hold you in high regard. You have marked my life, and for that, I will be eternally grateful to you. I love you, brother.

To Micky Mulero (Pai) And Nimsy López (Mai).

For bringing healing to the existing wounds of my heart. For taking the risk of bringing me to Puerto Rico and declaring over me: "Jesus heals you." For adopting me as your son. Due to the love you have shown me, I no longer feel like an orphan. I love you.

To my literature coach, Zoah Calveti.

In this life, the Holy Spirit links us to key people who will transport us towards excellence and help us achieve God's dream for you. When God revealed this book to me, I asked Him for His help. At a time when no one knew about this vision, God sent you to a Fruto de la Vid event in San Juan, Puerto Rico. There he told you about this book without knowing me. You were the instrument that the Lord used to bring to light the author who lived unconsciously in me. Thank you for being the guide and mentor of this book. You are a wonderful gift to the body of Christ, sent from heaven to assist people like me. Finally, I could silence the voice of that eighth-grade teacher who said to my mother: "Your son can't write." Thanks to you, today I am free from that negative influence. Shaina and I live eternally grateful for you and the love you have shown us throughout this beautiful journey of

"Hey Cancer! It's My Birthday Again".

To my Pastors Ephrain and Milca Padilla and to my entire Church: Iglesia de Dios Pentecostal MI Central Goldenrod, Orlando, Fl.

Thank you for welcoming me with open arms and always covering us in your prayers as we do God's work. I love you all.

To Pastor Barbara Santana and her beloved church Breaking the Yoke, Hainecity, Fl.

For standing out in the unconditional support of each project that our ministry undertakes. Thank you for every sowing of love. I love them.

To every person who has believed in this call and in some way or another have helped me to achieve the dream of being a preacher. You know who you are. I love you!

Finally, to all those who are battling against cancer today. Especially to every child fighting this disease. I will not give up! Instead, I will work even harder to bring more smiles to your hospital rooms while declaring that the sun will also rise again for you.

Book Reviews

The Evangelist Rafael "Nuni" Cuevas is a dynamic man of God. From birth, he was branded with the anointing of the Holy Spirit. Throughout his life, he has fought adversity, and despite everything, God has miraculously guarded him. These accounts are the indisputable truth of the Word of God. As stated in Hebrews 13:8, Jesus Christ is the same yesterday, today, and forever. Therefore, as you take this book in your hands, prepare yourself to feel the flow of the Holy Spirit knocking on the door of your heart, challenging you to believe in God above your adversities. Open your heart to receive a miracle in your life.

-Pastor Ephraim Padilla

From an early age, we observed a child who was very passionate about God's things. As we progressed throughout the years, we watched him face the processes and struggles that many others have encountered but could not withstand. For Nuni, it led to forming a young man whose intensity has never subsided, but burns today stronger than ever. His testimony is a living example that God's methods, although sometimes challenging, are meant to take you to another level of glory. By reading this book, your existence will change to a new degree of glorious life.

-Evangelista Andrés Cuevas

In the Christian life, God will always connect you with people of purpose who stimulate, encourage and challenge you. Meeting Rafael "Nuni" Cuevas was one of those divine relationships that bless and mark your life forever. "Nuni," as we affectionately call him, is a son of the house. Despite the processes he has undergone, we have seen his joy infecting everyone around him. We firmly believe that his testimony, which is embodied in this book, will be an injection of Faith that will mark your life. We do not doubt that this will only be the beginning of a beautiful path that God has already designed for His glory.

-Evangelist Micky Mulero and Nimsy López

Evangelist Rafael "Nuni" Cuevas is a dynamic and dedicated man of God. He is a man set apart for God to wreak havoc in the kingdom of darkness and do great things in the Kingdom of God. The enemy is terrified by the fact that this is a human being with a divine assignment. Since birth, the adversary has done everything possible to stop his life. This young preacher has lived a life of difficulties and trials that resembles the challenges in a work of art. He found himself trapped in darkness, cancer, and death at a young age, yet, even in his teens, he refused to give up. When adversity knocked on his door, the doctors gave up, the family was losing faith, the light of life was fading, and all that remained was for him to accept his fate and die.

Did something happen? Let me paraphrase Job 2:9-10 in relation to this powerful man of God: Doctors and skeptics said to him: "Are you still maintaining your integrity? Curse God and die!" But Nuni replied, "You are all talking like the foolish and the ignorant. Are we accepting the good of God and not the problems?" Today, his Faith is stronger than ever. Healed of cancer, he will boldly tell us: "I am limping so you can walk, and the scars on my body are here to remind you of the power, authenticity, and healing fire of the Holy Spirit!"

What you hold in your hands is not a book; it is a force that will paralyze all demonic diseases, schemes, and plans that have ever dared to rise up against you. I have never experienced more fire, power, and Holy Spirit preaching in my TBN Salsa program than with this mighty evangelist for the nations. So please sit back and enjoy this book because it is a journey into the supernatural realm. The place where heaven meets earth and light breaks the stronghold of darkness, disease, and death!

Pastor Edward Ramirez, Ed.S., M.S.O.L

Senior Pastor, Harvest Outreach Ministry

International Host: TBN Salsa, New York City

Table of Contents

Foreword

It is my great honor to write this foreword for a man who is so loved and close to my heart. Rafael (Nuni) Cuevas Jr. is my brother and my friend. His friendship endured despite the trials. I have known Nuni for more than twenty-three years. I feel incredibly blessed to be counted among his friends and watch him become a man of principle, integrity, and, above all, a man of God.

Nowadays, we can identify a worldwide abundance of ministries on altars, but few stand out in this era. Many people have heard of the price that one must pay and all that is necessary to sustain the mission. Some ministries have even sacrificed their personal lives, marriages, family, children, savings, and so much more to fulfill their calling and continue with their passion in life, which is to preach the gospel of Jesus Christ. This is the case of Nuni, who has not only rendered his life to carry the message of Jesus around the world, but has also dedicated himself amid a heavenly clash to fighting a battle against a disease, the same cancer that has affected millions of people globally.

Today, it is estimated that more than 20 million people will die of cancer annually by the year 2040. These astronomical projections come from the World Health Organization.

According to the above statistics, who would have imagined today that we would celebrate Rafael (Nuni) Cuevas Jr.? However, we now praise the Name of Jesus, who won the battle against cancer on behalf of our brother and friend. He saved him in order to save many others.

I will never forget the day when I first saw who I now know as this great man of God. Rafael (Nuni) Cuevas Jr. was just nine when we met. He was an extremely active boy. One night, when I arrived at his grandfather's church, where I was the invited preacher, I noticed this energetic little boy leading a group of children who ran rampant and caused chaos in the church. It's funny how at such a young age, he was already a person of influence. It caught my attention as I watched this group of children follow his every step and instruction. I also observed his grandfather, the Pastor of the Church, continually trying to berate Nuni to keep him calm and in line before starting the service. The most surprising thing was that when the service began, Nuni and his clan of misfits were very attentive to the music and who the guest speaker was, an unusual behavior among children.

After drawing my attention, the Lord began to speak to me. When I finished ministering the message to the church, I heard the word of the Lord Almighty instructing me to anoint this little boy. I can remember it as if it had just happened today, listening to the voice of God, subtle but clear as the day, telling me that Nuni would grow up to be a world-renowned evangelist. That he would carry the message of Jesus Christ to many nations, and God would manifest Himself in his ministry with signs and wonders. I obeyed God's instructions. As I called Nuni to the altar, I immediately proceeded to anoint his head with oil. Pastor Ramón Luis Hernández joined forces with me and prayed fervently for his grandson. As the tears ran down his cheeks, I heard him cry before the Lord in praise and adoration for choosing his grandson. What a great ministry!!

I was surprised to see this boy of nearly nine years old crying in the presence of God. Thus, I became a witness to the confirmation of his call when the Holy Spirit baptized Nuni with heavenly tongues at such a young age.

As the years passed, Nuni's ministry grew, signs and wonders followed him, just as God said. I felt fortunate to learn about Nuni's ministry and to hear people talk about how God's presence was with him wherever he went.

Life and its responsibilities took us in separate directions, even though we both continued to preach the Gospel of Jesus. But for some years, I knew nothing about where God had taken my brother and friend. Later, I found out my brother was fighting cancer. Anyone would wonder if the promises of God had come to an end in Nuni's life, yet we can be sure of this: the Word of God, the plan of God will be fulfilled, and no hell can prevent it.

In this powerful book full of faith, you will laugh, get angry and cry as you question God's infinite mind and why He allows some to traverse the depths of hell for the sake of others. The many years have taught me that God is there with each of us, even at our lowest level. When we are designated for such a special purpose, we will experience life, death, pain and will find ourselves struggling with problems beyond our understanding. In John 16:33, Jesus tells us: "These things I have spoken to you so that you may have peace in me. In the world, you will have affliction; but trust in me, I have conquered the world."

This book will lift your spirits as the author shares his experiences. This book will transform your life.

For those facing unimaginable problems, trials, and challenging times. For the ones currently dealing with depression. To the one who wonders if God will overcome. To you, the one who feels like there is no more fight in you. For the one who may have thrown in the towel. To all of you, I say: "Being convinced of this, that He who began a good work in you will carry it on to completion until the day of Jesus Christ." (Philippians 1:6, NIV).

When he was diagnosed with cancer, Nuni had many questions. Some of them were; What have I done to deserve this? Oh Lord, why have you forsaken me? What is behind this affliction? Will I ever get out of this? And although he had endless questions, a still voice within him continued to remind him that: "God is not a man, that He should lie, nor a son of man, that He should repent. Has He said, and will He not do? Or has He spoken, and will He not make it good?" (Numbers 23:19, NKJV).

Today, Nuni travels the world with his loving wife,

spreading the gospel and letting others know that if God says so, it will happen.

In closing, I wish to pray this prayer to our Lord Jesus Christ:

"My dear Heavenly Father, Savior, and Friend, I praise You for the life of my brother. I pray his testimony will reach millions of people through these means. I thank you for digging into the depths of this disease and rescuing him from an inevitable encounter with death. I pray that every person who needs to hear this word will be transformed and realize that Your love and kindness will go far beyond the limits of this world. I pray every reader will find You in each letter and all the experiences and details of this project. May this be one of the best stories that humanity has ever shared. In the Name which is above all names, we pray all this. The Name of our Lord and Savior Jesus Christ, and with the blessings of His Holy Spirit, Amen and Amen."

Humbly,

Prophet Carlos J. Ramirez

Introduction

From an early age, people have taught me that all the Glory belongs to God. That we should always render the Glory to Him. Nevertheless, I have come to understand that although men honor the Lord in saying "To God be the Glory," the reality is God is the sole proprietor of the Glory. Whether we give it up or not, the Glory already belongs to Him, and He will always retain it. Granted, I understand and exercise the principle of continually giving God the Glory; it is one of the things that I practice the most. Still, what can we present to God that He doesn't already have? A while back, I asked myself this question. What can we offer Him that He is not already the owner of it? Thankfulness! Gratitude belongs to us, and we deliver it to whoever we desire.

The Bible speaks of ten lepers that Jesus healed, but only one of them returned to thank Him. I try to live my life as that single leper since many others have survived cancer yet have forgotten who their healer was. They never testify about it, much less thank Jesus for it. So today, I thank my Lord Jesus. Not only for dying on the Cross for me but also for having cured me of terminal cancer. If Jesus had not healed me, I would never have experienced such beautiful blessings. Including the blessing of finding a beautiful wife, having many nephews, and living the precious privilege of taking this beautiful gospel to the world. The crowds do not impress me; what strikes me is knowing that God noticed me so that I would carry out His will. I don't know what He saw in me, but I am sure of what I've seen in Him.

At the end of April 2018, minutes before I began the book you are holding today, I spoke on the phone with Zoah Calveti. Her words intrigued me. Before praying for me so that the Holy Spirit would take control of all writing, her advice was: "Nuni, when you are writing, there will come times when you will cry. When that happens, stop writing and cry, because it is God who is healing your heart. "As I listened to her, I did not understand why I would cry, since it had been ten years since my cancer. I felt entirely healed from everything.

However, I wish the printing company that printed this beautiful book had a special machine that could publish every word, along with every tear that fell on my computer as I wrote each chapter. Having said that, I feel in the spirit to give you my encourager's advice. While you read this book, there will come times when you will also cry. When this happens, just cry. Let God heal the wounds which He has made known in you, because Jesus heals you.

They say there are two critical moments in the life of a human being; the day you are born, and the day one discovers purpose. Some people claim not to have a purpose in life, or perhaps they have yet to find it. It is my prayer that as you read this book, you can enter not only into a deep relationship with God but that you can discover your mission in life. The Bible says: "For where your treasure is, there your heart will be also" (Luke 12:34). If there is something that I am sure of, it is that, wherever there is a big "X," there is a great treasure underneath. If people or circumstances have put an "X" in your life, get ready because you have immense riches hidden within you. God will soon reveal it and bring it to light. Get ready to shine! Because your life has much value.

It is my earnest petition that as you cross each letter of this work that the Holy Spirit be with you. I am confident in this one thing, as you navigate the pages of this book, God will deal with you in a unique and special way. Last but not least, it is my wish that you follow these instructions. During your reading time, please keep your mind and heart open. Don't let doubt disconnect you from the beautiful journey that God has prepared for you through this book. This final instruction is most important: <u>You should not read this book without first reading Chapter 28.</u> I know I might be asking for something out of the ordinary, but this last chapter, intended to provide a prophetic perspective, will provide hope even in the darkest moments of this text. As I told you before, "God will deal with you in a unique and special way." So let's begin this extraordinary journey: Please proceed to Chapter 28 before reading Chapter 1.

ATTENTION!

DO NOT PROCEED
WITHOUT FIRST
READING CHAPTER 28

Chapter 1

A Mother's Prayer

In the living room of a humble home, my mother prayed. Pregnant with me, she was fasting even at seven months. So it was; before my birth, my mom was already fasting and praying for the fruit of her womb. She appeared before the Lord with a special request. In those days, there were no famous "Gender Reveal Parties" where families and friends get together to discover the sex of a baby. There were also no black, confetti-filled balloons ready with the colors blue or pink to announce whether she was a boy or a girl. In the past, everything was a big surprise. In her request to God, my mother said: "Lord, I don't know if this child is female or male, I only know that although I already have a girl, I will receive with joy whatever you give me. But if you grant me a son, I ask that he be an evangelist, who can take Your Word to the whole world". Immediately after expressing those words to the Lord, at that very moment, I began jumping in her womb, and this confirmed in her spirit that God had already answered her request.

My mother describes how out of the three births she had, mine was the fastest and easiest. Although the doctor rushed to attend to her, I was born without his help upon arriving at the hospital. I was eager to begin living God's purpose for my life. If there is one thing I can assure you, it is that I love life.

And so it all began. On May 18, 1985, at Beth Israel Hospital in Newark, NJ, Rafael Cuevas Jr., better known as Nuni, was born. The only son of Rafael and Lourdes Cuevas. I think every detail of what happened at my birth was prophetic, from my mother's fast to the hospital's name, even as far as the name which, thanks to my father, was given to me.

For me, it has always been a great honor to carry my father's name and honor him as the only male in his house. In everything, I have recognized this privilege as something noteworthy. Whenever my name is mentioned, whether on a stage or in front of thousands of people, on television, or even in this book, I feel like he is also being proclaimed. With that said, I continually bear in mind the great responsibility of properly representing his name. I consider that everything that I have achieved for the Glory of God, he has also reached for the Glory of God.

For as long as I can remember, I have always felt a special connection with my dad. My dad was the kind of father who constantly caressed his children, showing us a lot of love and affection. I am the middle child, the only male between two females. My sister Yajaira is the eldest by a year and a half. I am four years older than my little sister, Rosa, better known as Fanny. My father was the type to always come home from work with great joy. From the moment he opened the door, he called each of us with a unique whistle. Yes, my dad is quite a character! He spoke to us through whistling. Depending on his whistle's tone, we understood who he was referring to and even what he meant to say through his whistling. This was a daily routine.

My mom was a housewife. She cared for the children while Dad worked. By the time he would arrive, the house was always clean, and dinner was served. All seemed to be perfect, just like in a fairy tale. When I was four years old, I began to notice a change. Not everything was going well. As the very attentive child that I was, I realized that my mom and dad were not getting along like they used to. Suddenly there were many fights between them. Daily, at least one of my toys would disappear. And if it wasn't one of my toys, something else of great value in the house would disappear. Back then, because of my early age, I could not know or understand that my dad was fighting a monster called heroin.

At that same age, I remember when I began to see things at night, black shadows that flew through the living room of my house, which did not allow me to sleep. They caused me much fright and fear. I longed to see the dawn in the darkness of the night since all torture disappeared when the sun rose. Each day I wished that nightfall would never come, for I knew those shadows would return to haunt me.

One particular night clearly comes to mind when we were all sleeping in my parents' room. It was a hot summer day. In our tiny apartment, my parents' bedroom was the only place with air conditioning. So that we would not suffer from the heat, my mother would gather us to sleep with them. That same night when everyone fell asleep, I observed a man, whose height reached the ceiling, coming into our room and standing next to the bed where my dad was sleeping. My little heart was beating at full speed. I had a feeling that this character was not at all good. He was staring at my dad all night long. This figure wore a black hat and dressed in a long black jacket that stretched down to his feet. Every night, for a whole week, I watched him appear in what I described as an invisible elevator. Revealing himself, he would park next to my dad, watching over him throughout the night. He kept his eyes fixed on him until the sunrise. At dawn, as the sun would rise, that man in the black cap descended on his invisible elevator. I would immediately get out of my blanket to see where he was going, but by the time I could look, the man had already disappeared, and my dad would wake up.

After repeatedly living this episode for a week, I couldn't take it anymore, and one morning I told my parents about it over breakfast. My dad was eating, and when he heard what I was telling him, his face changed color. His appetite was gone, especially since my mother had shared a dream about him a few minutes prior. In her dream, she saw how some men kidnapped him and took him to an abandoned building to kill him. Towards the end of the dream, she saw how they tied him to a chair, covered his face, and then "gunned him down," which means they murdered him.

Quickly he understood that death was stalking him. Both of my parents knew the Word of God, although, after my birth, they separated from Him. When they stopped attending church, they gave entrance to this man in a black hat. However, whenever heaven has a plan with you, hell cannot stop it. I wholeheartedly believe that the most significant sign that points towards a life that carries a powerful divine plan is that, even when the person is unaware of their purpose, the man in a black hat is already visiting their home.

Before Moses was born, Pharaoh was already looking to kill him. Similarly, Jesus had barely been born when Herod, just like Pharaoh, also sought to kill him. Your enemy has a plan, but beyond that plan, there is the one who wrote our story long before you and I could live it. Today, you have the opportunity to read it and believe it: "no weapon formed against you will prosper" (Isaiah 54:17, NIV).

There was a man named Noah who lived in my neighborhood. He drove the church bus and always went throughout the community evangelizing. I still remember watching him preach in the streets and hearing the sound of his voice as he shouted, "Jesus." Noah always preached without shame. There is always at least one person who is committed to carrying a message of faith and hope among our communities. Many times they end up being ignored by those who feel no need to hear about God or the church. My dad was one among the people who fled from Noah whenever they noticed him through the neighborhood. "The wicked flee without being pursued" (Proverbs 28: 1, NIV).

One afternoon Noah ran into my parents and asked their permission to take my sister Yajaira and me to Bible school. For the first time in our lives, we both went to church. It was a Sunday morning, and every person in that room was singing praises. I could not understand what was happening, but Noah, with great joy, sang a chorus that said: "The blond man from Galilee is passing by. Let Him touch you, let Him touch you, receive His blessing." Amid that praise, Noah began to shout, "Jesus is here. Jesus is here. Let him touch you." Still, in my mind and my heart, I can hear Noah's voice. I also remember listening to the accompanying guitar and the sisters playing the tambourines. Within the praise, I felt a supernatural presence. My body hairs began standing up; my whole being trembled, not because of fear or coldness, but because of the perceived presence in that place.

Unaware of what was happening, I looked to my side for the moment because I felt the presence of someone standing nearby. As I watched, I saw glittering sandals and a white robe over them. I closed my eyes and said, "Who is that?" Noah stopped singing only to whisper in my ear, "Nuni, Jesus is next to you; ask Him to touch you!" Instantly I began to cry because I felt something touching me. It was so powerful and beautiful that it filled me with joy, peace, and love. The fear within me, the one caused by the shadows tormenting me at night, fell under the control of that presence. At only four years old, I did as Noah told me and started saying, "Jesus touch me. Jesus touch me. Please touch me! Touch daddy, please don't let the man in the black hat take him away. Touch my mommy too, because she cries a lot."

Several days later, my dad was walking into church with me. An older woman with white hair came from Puerto Rico to preach that night. While she was ministering the word, that woman turns to my dad to impart a message from God. Pointing to him, she says: "Death is surrounding you, but God has a plan for your life." My father couldn't resist any longer, and that same night he gave his heart to Jesus. That older woman put her hands on him, and my dad was instantly free. It would be difficult for any four-year-old to explain what God was doing at the time, but I managed to understand that our lives would change.

And so it happened, things began to change in my home. There were no more fights like before. Shortly after seeing a change in my dad, my mother also gave herself to Jesus. Perhaps, you are reading this and thinking: "This is not for me. I don't believe in religion". I want you to know that I do not believe in religions either, as they have been the cause of many wars and great divisions in the world. Religion is guilty of the condemnation of millions of people. Plus, I believe in Jesus! Jesus is not a religion based on one-sided demands. Jesus is a mutual experience. He is salvation, deliverance, and healing. And more than all that, He loves us and longs to befriend all of humanity. If you are reading this book, it is because Jesus wants to have a relationship with you just as he has had it with me.

As I was saying, everything at home had changed. Now there was peace in our home. I stopped seeing the man with the black hat and those shadows which often visited at night. Now, as dusk came, I slept like a baby. A short time after my dad's conversion, he became a deacon of the church. He started studying at a theological seminary until he became a teacher in that institute. I observed my dad a lot. I paid attention to the way he spoke and the way he dressed. I noticed that he was gifted in public speaking and expressing himself in an awe-inspiring way; I wanted to be like him.

At the age of six, I had a vision. My bedroom was in an attic, and there, in that room, the Lord visited me. In the vision, I saw myself as a grown man, just as I am today, preaching to thousands of people all over the world. I found myself on grand stages, watching myself praying for the sick and they would heal. Within all this, I heard a mighty voice that simultaneously filled me with much peace. It was the voice of God. I was hearing it for the first time. He told me: "Nuni, I have chosen you to preach my Word. You will be a prophet to the nations. You will pray for the sick, and they will heal. You will be an evangelist ".

It was a Sunday morning when I woke up from that vision. For the past two years, it became a habit; my mom would be the one to wake the whole family to go to Bible School. Although mom had separated a pair of jeans and a shirt for me, I started fighting with her because I didn't want to wear those clothes. Like a typical Latin mother, she already had the flip-flop in her hand, ready to strike me. I said, "Please, Mommy, don't let me go to church like this. Let me put on the blazer that I have in my closet". We were not rich, nor were we poor. We had just enough to survive. The overcoat that I was referring to was the only one I had. My mom, not understanding why I insisted on dressing like this, finally asked the question; "Why do you want to go to church like this?" I replied: "Last night I dreamed that I was an evangelist and I am going to be an evangelist.".

My mom looked at me with an astonished face because she had never told me, or anyone else, the request that she made to God when she was pregnant with me. It may be that up to this point, she had forgotten her prayer, but God never forgets His promises. From that day on, every Sunday, I started going to church in the same black coat. I would carry my large Bible under my arm. The truth is that it was not really a Bible, but a children's book, with a variety of biblical stories, told in pictures. That was my first Bible, and I carried it with great pride. I didn't know how, but I was sure that I would be a preacher one day.

My dad came to preach one Sunday, and I was captivated by his preaching style. I had never seen it done that way. While he preached, he made you live what he was saying, managing to capture all the public's attention. That amazed me, and I said to myself: "This is how I want to preach!" I would always sit in the first pew of the church because I was an evangelist. Allow me to explain; in all actuality, I was still a child. But as much as people saw a child, I viewed myself as a preacher. So I spoke like a preacher. I walked with my cartoon Bible under my arm, like a preacher. Even though nobody understood me, I understood me.

Every day, while I was at home, I would arrange all of my sisters' stuffed animals so that I could preach to them. I held services with them. I would preach to them and then lay my hands on them, praying for each one. On the sly, my mom watched me in action. Laughing, she told my family all about it, not jokingly, but rather out of joy, knowing that her son was attracted to the call of a preacher. You will never achieve your dreams if you don't start walking and talking, just as you have dreamt.

At that time, we lived in a two-story house. Above our apartment resided a lady named Socorro. One afternoon Socorro came screaming from migraine pains. She returned from the hospital, where they tried to treat her migraine, but it still hadn't gone away. My mom desperately brings her into our house and, sitting her on the couch, starts screaming: "Nuni, Nuni!" I was in my room, in the middle of my daily sermon. I walked out of the bedroom towards my mom, only to find Socorro screaming and crying, tormented by a migraine. My mother asked me to watch Socorro while she searched the kitchen, attempting to find some remedy that she could give her. As soon as my mother left the living room, I began to climb onto the sofa where Socorro was agonizing. I managed to stand next to her. Placing my hands upon her head, I said, "Migraine, in the name of Jesus, get out of her!" At that exact moment, Socorro, with a single cry, fell on the floor and fell asleep.

My mom hurried into the room, only to experience that scene. Hand to mouth, she couldn't believe what she was seeing. After a few minutes, Socorro got up from the floor, and my mother poured her a glass of water. In her amazement, Socorro could not even speak. After a few minutes, she looked at us and said: "The pain I had is gone." Joyfully, Socorro kissed and hugged me because she was cured of the migraine. At that very moment, my mother understood that I had an extraordinary calling, that I was not an average child, and I needed special care.

Chapter 2

Divine Protection

In the previous chapter, I shared that when God has a plan with you, hell will always do everything in its power to stop it. Clearly, God established that there was a special calling upon my life. I was a child carrying a supernatural calling. Like every boy, I loved playing. I had an incredible imagination. At this moment, I still maintain the same creativity, even within the vision of God for my life. I genuinely believe "nothing is impossible." I rely much more on that statement than on the words: "You can't." Impossibility stands as a challenge that will provoke the best of me.

Between the 1980s and 1990s, my parents were raising us in Newark, New Jersey, one of the worst cities in existence. There they suffered many crimes, murders, drug dealings, and car thefts.

One Sunday morning, my father and I walked hand in hand to church. Suddenly, a car jumped onto the sidewalk where we moved along and drove directly towards us at high speed. It looked as if it was going to crush us. Swiftly, at the last second, just as the car was about to run us over, he jumped back on the road and continued at an even faster speed until we could no longer see him.

That same night, my father and I went to a restaurant near my house to buy a meal. As Dad made his request, a young man came to us. Crying, he said, "Please, I want you to forgive me." My troubled father asked why he would have to forgive him if we didn't know him. The young man tells my father that he was with his friends under the influence of drugs and alcohol on that morning. As he was leaving a party with his also drugged-up friends, they told him: "Run over that man and his child." He confessed to my dad that he intended to trample over us. That he didn't really want to do it, but something in him drove him. He also had the added pressure of his intoxicated friends, prompting him to tread over us with his car.

The most striking thing about his story was not that he confessed his impulse to crush us, but what he said next. "When I drove the car over the sidewalk where you walked, I noticed a giant standing in front of you. He was wearing white clothes, and with his finger, he told me no!" Weeping, he recounted how he immediately drove his car back onto the road. The young man also said that his friends started yelling at him. They asked, "What happened? Why didn't you do it?" But when he told them what he witnessed, they started making fun of him, saying that he must have imagined it due to the drugs. But the young man insisted, "I know what I saw... It was not the drugs. You are walking with a giant dressed in white, and I saw him". So the young man ran out of the restaurant, and we never saw him again. My father hugged me and said: "That giant is the angel of Jehovah!" Then, I understood that I had an enemy, but also a protector.

My parents came from Ponce, Puerto Rico, neither had Christian parents. Their upbringing was very different from mine. Both were born and raised in unsafe neighborhoods. Many Latinos and African-Americans can relate to me when I say that our parents can be pretty intense at the time of correction. When it comes to unleashing the belt, they don't hesitate. As I disclosed at the beginning of this chapter, I was an imaginative child, which caused me many problems at home. I loved jumping on my mother's furniture and the bedroom mattress. I thought I was a "Ninja Turtle," a "Power Ranger," or even a "WWE" fighter.

I was never a child who was inclined to do harm or evil. Rather, my scoldings were due to the fact that I was never still, or sometimes because I had received an order I had yet to fulfill. Whenever the above-mentioned circumstances would occur, I faced a beating with the belt or whatever my parents could find at the time. However, I don't blame them since that's what they learned as the proper correction. Of the three kids at home, I was the one who got the most beatings and punishments. So, I guess what they say about the middle child is true...

Currently, in my adulthood, I believe in correction, but not in the same way that my parents practiced. I consider that while reprimanding a child is necessary, there are many alternatives that do not have to lead to physical contact. Such punishments can be; a timeout in their bedroom, taking away toys, or even prohibiting the use of electronic devices, including telephones, gaming stations, and iPads. The solution is not to strike the child with an object or to obtain a doctor's prescription so that your child is high all day long. You're dealing with a child and not an animal. If we can ensure animals have rights to protect them from such acts, how much more should a child be preserved? Above all, we must consider that every human being must first be a child before becoming an adult.

Most of the time, my dad was the one who disciplined me. Whenever he did so, he was blinded to the point of leaving marks on my body. Perhaps in his anger, he forgot that I was a just a kid and not a man on the street who wanted to hurt him. As I have previously told you, I don't blame them because it was what they learned at home. Even so, with all of his mistreatments, there was only love for him in me. So much so that after correcting me, I would search the whole house for him to see if he wanted to play or watch a movie with me. People tend to think that because someone serves Jesus, they are the perfect person. On the contrary, those of us who serve Jesus do so because we understand that our imperfections will lead us to perdition, and only through Jesus will we receive forgiveness and salvation.

John 3:16 (KJV)

For God so loved the world that he gave his only begotten Son, so that everyone who believes in him may not perish, but may have eternal life.

Ephesians 4:13 (KJV)

Until we all come to the unity of the Faith and the knowledge of the Son of God, to a perfect man, to the measure of the stature of the fullness of Christ.

Anyone who commits themselves to a relationship with Jesus enters into a maturing process leading towards becoming as He was on earth. After all, my dad had only been in the Gospel for a few brief years and was still developing as a Christian. In this case, Jesus would deal with him in such a way that he would become more tolerant of me. I often wonder: "If Jesus is patient with us, why can't we be patient with others?" Especially when patience is one of the most important fruit of the Spirit, necessary for a person to grow in a relationship with Jesus.

Since our family was the largest, all family events were regularly held at our home. While the adults ate and talked in the living room, all my cousins would gather in the basement of the house, where we played and watched TV. Once during a family gathering, I was in my room, preparing to join my cousins in the basement. I had recently come out of the shower when they were already playing in the basement. I was the only one missing. During one of their games, someone accidentally broke through the wall and created a large hole. Now keep in mind that while all this is happening, I am in my room getting dressed. When I finally went downstairs, all my cousins started running, and I ended up entering the basement at the same time they left. As I turned around, my dad was standing behind me. I distinctly remember his shouts. He grabbed me by the neck until I almost ran out of breath. Then he took off his belt and started hitting me with it. My dad was a very strong man, and he did not measure his strength when he would strike us. Fury blinded him. When he finished with me, I could no longer walk. His leather strap marked my entire body. I can clearly recall my mother's cry when she found me on the basement floor, injured and sobbing.

For this reason, I didn't go to school for a week. We were afraid that some teachers would notice my marks and then have my father arrested. That night I remember getting on my knees to pray. I was only eight years old, but in tears, I asked God if He could talk to my dad, so he would never hit me that way again. A week later, in the middle of the night, my dad woke me up. Filled with tears, he cried out for forgiveness. Later, he explained that while he slept, an angel visited him, saying: "God is upset with you because you hurt His anointed one. Thus says the Lord to you: The next time you put your hands in the same way upon God's anointed, you will cease to live. The Lord will take your life. For the Lord has given you a prophet who will spread the Word of God throughout the world, and it is your responsibility to take good care of him." From that day on, my dad was much more patient with me. He was no longer hitting me with the force or violence in which he used to.

Just because my dad hit me the way he did, it didn't mean he didn't love me. He loved me enough and wished better for me; therefore, he applied correction. The problem came with unnecessary punishment and moments with too much force. Or, like in this particular case, chastising without actually knowing what happened and who was responsible.

Perhaps as you read all this, you may say: "¿Divine Protection? ¿Where was it?" Every person carrying a Divine Purpose also has Divine Protection. I explain. Purpose is the reason; in this case, it is the reason why we exist.

"Before I formed you in the womb I knew you, and before you were born I sanctified you, I gave you as a prophet to the nations."
(Jeremiah 1: 5 KJV)

Each individual on this planet has a purpose; however, this fact does not exclude us from experiencing painful moments. No one promised us a life absent of abuse. Having a purpose does not mean that we exist inside a globe where nobody can touch us. Jesus came to earth and left us a Word for the most challenging times. He said: "These things I have spoken to you so that you may have peace in me. In the world you will have affliction, but be of good cheer, I have overcome the world" (John 16:33, RVR1960).

We can identify, as clearly stated, that within our lives, hardship will come. Occasions of injustice will approach us, and we will face situations that will mark and hurt us. But even in the midst of all this, God's protection will be present. Please take a moment to consider all the past difficulties and how much pain they have caused you. Remember those moments of grief that perhaps left their scars behind. They scarred you but could not kill you. If all these circumstances failed to eliminate you, it is because you still carry a purpose that will remain in you until fulfilled. A purpose far more powerful than any suffering you can bear.

Start thinking about all those people who have died from situations of less impact than your past. Things that shouldn't lead to death. But you, with all the seriousness of what you have lived, are still here reading this book. It is so because God is not finished with you; you still have His Divine Protection. God does not allow death to touch us until His divine purpose is fulfilled in our lives. Through Jesus, we will be able to conquer those moments of pain and affliction. If Jesus overcame, then we will also overcome. It's the reason you survived the car accident. Even though the car was a total loss, you came out with your life intact. If you are still alive, you have divine protection. Or, perhaps, your house suffered a fire where everything in the home burned, but the flames of fire failed to touch your life. What's more, who says that the abuse or whatever has caused you so much pain in life is not precisely what God will use so that today you become the powerful instrument that you are to be.

You intended to harm me, but God intended it for good to accomplish what is now being done, the saving of many lives.
(Genesis 50:20, NIV)

The enemy of our souls sometimes manages to

cause us a lot of pain, but God turns suffering into a force, to transform us into what we are today or what we will be tomorrow. So instead of playing the role of a victim, celebrate! Although they deliberately sent that attack to kill or destroy you, your divine protection intervened. This next powerful verse complements this chapter nicely:

When you pass through the waters, I will be with you; and when you pass through the rivers, they will not sweep over you. When you walk through the fire, you will not be burned; the flames will not set you ablaze.
(Isaiah 43:2, NIV)

Once again, the Word of God confirms that yes, you will have moments of affliction and face storms in your life, but they will not destroy you. On the contrary, they will make you stronger, especially since God will be with you throughout the entire process. Have peace and trust that this is not your end.

Chapter 3

Nobody Wants to Believe Me

I lived with the knowledge that God had chosen me for greatness. Because of the dream where the voice of God called me, I knew that I carried a significant purpose in me, that I would grow and be a person of great inspiration for the world. But people did not believe me. Many criticized me for the way I was, mainly because I stopped talking like a child to express myself as an adult. My friends were always people much older than me. In any case, I wanted to act older than I really was. Noticing that even the surrounding children did not understand me, I sought to belong to the youth group.

While my friends wanted to play Nintendo and hide-and-seek, my desire was to preach. But I was just a kid. If I could go back in time and visit that child, I would say, "There is nothing wrong with being a boy. Don't be in such a hurry to grow up, for everything has its time. Above all, I assure you that God will take care of realizing your dream, but, at the same time, I warn you that you should not tell everyone about it. I'll ask you to stop living trying to prove to everyone that you once had a dream. Instead, focus on establishing with your life that what God said about you is true."

People who have never achieved greatness or any significant thing in life can hear you talk about what God will do with you but are incapable of receiving it. Since they cannot rejoice over the goal that lies ahead of you, they lend themselves to criticism and ridicule. The truth is that a large part of them wants to be like you, but they know they can't. Deep down, they're nothing but admirers with their hearts full of evil. Instead of trying to help you achieve your dream, they try to stop it. If only they knew that by supporting you in your goals, they are sowing a seed of acceleration so their dreams can also come true. In the following case, this happened even faster than usual.

The book of Exodus states that when Pharaoh heard that God was going to provide a deliverer among the Hebrew men through a firstborn, he wanted to use the midwives to stop Him. Historical records prove that Pharaoh specifically requested these midwives to be sterile. When Hebrew women gave birth, the order was clear; if the baby was a boy, they must kill him. In his thought process, Pharaoh believed that these midwives, out of envy, would not allow others to give birth to a child. These women had never been able to conceive, let alone give birth, so Pharaoh intended to use jealousy to drive them to the point of murdering the very thing that they would never obtain. One of the enemy's most common strategies is to arouse envy among our own people since jealousy is the same effective blinding emotion that led him to betray his own God (Ezekiel 28: 12-19). The Bible says those midwives refused to obey Pharaoh; therefore, God's favor manifested upon them. For having helped those Hebrew women achieve their dream of being mothers, God blessed them and healed their wombs. When you become a partner for others to accomplish God's dream, you will also discover His blessing manifested in your life. Everything previously impossible to achieve, the favor of God will ordain it possible.

At the age of nine, in the fourth grade, there was a bully at school. All the students were afraid of him because that boy even intimidated the teachers. So much so that I dare say they also hated him. He was always doing bad things, and no one could correct him. For a child, he showed much cruelty in his heart. One day, that bully challenged me to fight; since I did not accept, he gave me the beating of the century. As I was leaving school, he attacked me; he took my face and swept it against all the snow that existed on the street. When my dad came to pick me up, he found me all wounded, with my face cut up by the snow. To top it all off, my friend told my father that I refused to defend myself. When my father asked me why I did not protect myself, my answer was: "I am an evangelist, and Jesus said if someone hits me, my duty is to give him the other side of my face." I think my answer bothered him a lot more than seeing my beaten face. Of course, no parent wants to witness a child hurt, much less because someone feels like abusing him. I remember when I got home, my dad called all my uncles and even my foster grandfather, who was my pastor.

They all came to my house asking me once again why I did not defend myself. Hearing my answer, everyone got mad at me. To give you a little more background, my dad and my uncles practiced boxing as a sport. Solely for lack of discipline, they never became professionals. They had taught me how to defend myself since we even had a gym and a boxing ring in the basement of a building that my foster grandfather attended. When they saw my bruises, they were confused, unable to understand why I would not fight that bully. Suddenly my grandfather, full of anger, shouts: "You are not an evangelist, so tomorrow you will go to school, and you are going to beat up that bully because you know how to box!" His response hit me harder than the bully's blows. I would have preferred the punches of that intimidator instead of hearing from the mouth of a minister that God had no purpose with me. Hearing the words: "You are not an evangelist" was equivalent to him saying to me: "You do not have a calling from God." The truth was that yes, I knew how to fight, and I was not afraid of the boy, but more than anything, I loved God and did not want to offend Him. Above all, I knew and understood that God is a God of peace and not of strife. In the same way, I figured if I fought, I would ruin his plans to one day be an evangelist.

The next day, I got up in the morning and said to God: "Father God, I have to fight at school today. If I don't fight, I will have a big problem with my dad, grandfather, and uncles. I ask you to forgive me and that after this, I can continue to be an evangelist". In my innocence, I came to believe that I would lose the ministry and the gifts that God had for me, that this fight was going to ruin God's plan for

40

me. The reality is many adults have failed God, and today they still think as I did when I was a child. They consider that God will take away their gifts or even His calling because they have committed a fault. Yet our gifts are irrevocable; once God gives them, He never takes them away (see Romans 11:29). The Bible speaks of great men of God who at some point failed. Adam, Noah, Abraham, even the Apostle Peter who denied Jesus, not just once, but three times. Even so, Jesus appears to him after his resurrection and says: "Feed my sheep" (John 21:17, ESV).

To be clear, I do not establish this principle as a license for you to fail God as many times as you please. Rather, so that you may understand that the purpose of God for your life goes above your mistakes. When God called Abraham, He knew that in his heart there was an Ishmael. This matter is not about your mistakes; it is about purpose. In all this, I learned that although we are human beings prone to failing Him, God will never fail us. He always keeps His promises. If God said it, He will do it, even above your mistakes. Your success is not determined by what you've done but rather by what God said you would do.

I remember arriving at my school, and at lunchtime, my dad showed up. He approached me and said: "You are going to fight, and I am here to defend you from your teachers and the school principal." You can imagine the nervous tension I was experiencing at that moment. My hands were sweating, and my heart was beating so fast. All my friends asked: "Rafael, are you really going to fight? Followed by, "...But aren't you a Christian, Rafael?" I answered them all by saying: "You're right. I am a Christian, but the Bible also tells me that I have to honor my parents. And my dad wants me to beat up this bully. "

We went into the school cafeteria. All the children were lining up to get their lunch. As they organized themselves, they were saying, "Rafael is going to fight today." My God, that was like announcing Mayweather was going to fight Pacquiao. All the children were waiting to see what would happen since they were all aware that I was a Christian and had never fought with anyone. I always got along well with all my schoolmates and with my classroom teachers. I never missed an opportunity to tell them about Jesus.

My dad stood in a corner and yelled at me: "Here it comes! Now we're talking!" The bully stood in front of me and challenged me once again. All the children stopped eating only to witness what was going to happen. Perhaps you think that this is the part of the story where an angel appears. Well, guess what? I was also waiting for an angel to reveal himself to that bully, but no one appeared. So, I took the stance of a professional boxer which confused the bully. When he threw the first punch, I ducked, and my dad shouted, "Jab, jab, right, hook," so that's what I did. When I looked down, the bully was on the ground and could not react. All the children were screaming because someone finally confronted him.

You could hear the applause and shouts of the children, even from the adults who worked in the cafeteria. My dad hugged me and lifted me as if I had won a championship. I felt just like in the movie Rocky 4 when Rocky Balboa beat the Russian. The only thing missing was someone to set the United States flag over me.

But when I saw the bully knocked out on the ground and unresponsive, I heard an evil voice that said to me: "You killed him. Instead of winning him for Christ, you surrendered him to hell. You are no longer an evangelist." Yes, at the young age of 9, I was living that episode in my life. I started to cry. "Daddy, I killed him. Daddy, NO!" All of a sudden, the bully was lifted, and he began to recover. Can you imagine the relief I felt?

Consequently, my dad, the bully, and I ended up at the school principal's office. The truth is while I was walking to the office, even though the children shouted: "You won, you won!" I felt horrible. It seemed to me like God was grieved with me, and just thinking about that made my heart ache. I figured that I was no longer going to be an evangelist.

Have you ever heard of "love at first sight?" It is the moment when a boy sees the love of his life for the first time, immediately falling in love with her, becoming incapable of resisting being excited about her. Imagine this, and you will better understand how I felt when God showed me His will for my life. I was in love and excited. But now, in one sad moment, I sensed I had lost the love of my life. Preaching the Word of God became a fantasy that would never happen for me.

Following the meeting with the school principal, the bully was suspended, and I was congratulated on winning. They gave me the rest of the afternoon free to go home with my dad. As soon as my dad got home, with great joy, he told everyone how his son fought back and knocked out the school bully. He also told them how the school principal did not discipline me for what happened but instead congratulated me and even gave me the rest of the afternoon off. Right away, my dad started making plans with me. He told me: "You are going to become a good boxer. We are going to start training you. "Without delay, my dad bought all the equipment I needed to box. He even found the people who would work with me. I cried, pleading with him: "No, daddy, I'm going to be an evangelist," but his response was: "What? An evangelist! No, not an evangelist! You're going to be a boxer!" I remember going into my room to talk to God and asking Him, "Why did you allow me to fight? Why didn't an angel appear? I want to live what I dreamed of. I want to be an evangelist". God did not send me an angel, but he did send me a prophet.

The fight happened on Tuesday, and, as usual, on the following Sunday, we arrived at church for service. During the car ride, my dad told me that he had everything ready to start boxing; that same week, we would begin training. However, there was still a great sadness inside me. When we entered the Church, I knelt to pray, as always. Since no one wanted to believe that I had a calling to be an evangelist, in my prayer, I asked God to speak for me. That night, a young prophet named Carlos Ramírez Jr., better known as Carlitos, was our guest speaker. As he preached, I said within me: "I want to be like him, but nobody believes me." This young man carried a powerful anointing, accompanied by many gifts. Prophet Carlos Ramírez Jr. was one of the first evangelists I have ever witnessed calling people by name, surname, and even social security number. Wherever he went, God performed amazing miracles.

That night, he called various people by their names, and as he prayed for the sick, God would heal them. At the time of the altar call, I went forward, saying within my heart: "I want to be like that young man. I want what he has." During his preaching, I noticed he did it precisely how I had visualized myself preaching in my dream. I wanted him to pray for me, and maybe through his prayer, God would give me one more chance to become an evangelist. As I walked down the aisle, I clearly remember a woman saying to me: "What are you coming for? Go back to your seat. Can't you see they are praying for the people?" What I experienced at that moment was very similar to the instance when Jesus had to say to his disciples:

"Let the little children come to Me, and do not forbid them; for of such is the kingdom of God."

(Luke 18:16, NKJV)

When I turned around to go back to my seat, Carlitos called me and asked me to come over to him. As I came before him, I was broken and trembling before God because the Holy Spirit was touching me. He asked about my parents, so they stood next to me. It was then, in front of everyone, where he said to me on behalf of God: "You are going to put on your boxing gloves, but it is to fight the devil and his empire." Looking at my dad, he continued: "This week the enemy had a trap for this child, but today God breaks that trap. He is not a boxer. He is an evangelist". Immediately my parents began to cry while that prophet of God gave them instructions so that they would take good care of me. He then tells me: "This is what the Lord says to you: You will travel and preach my Word throughout the nations. You will pray for the sick, and they will heal. You will be a great inspiration to the world by bringing Faith to those who no longer have it. Many will come to Jesus through you". Instantly, as confirmation that God was the one speaking, a glory fell upon all the people

47

who heard the message.

Then the prophet anointed me with oil and presented me to God. That same night Carlitos had me pray for the crowd before him. For the first time, in that moment, I finally felt like everyone believed in the calling that God had for my life. People even asked me to lay my hands on them and pray for them. When God has a greater purpose for your life, He will release a Word on your behalf, which will be enough to encourage you. That same declaration will trail-blaze pathways in your favor that will lead you towards achieving the complete realization of that promise.

By the time I got home, I was elated. The joy was so great that I couldn't sleep. I was lying on my bed, staring at the ceiling, imagining myself traveling the world, carrying a message of Faith and hope. In that scene, I could see my future life; preaching the Word of God with power, praying for the sick, and watching them get well.

What I could not know was how much it was going to cost me…

Chapter 4
Training

In life, everything has its time, and everything has a waiting period. When a woman hears the news that she will be a mother, she enters into nine months of expectation. During that period of time, her womb and the child within her begin to undergo changes. These changes are more like developments. Every week and every month, the child enters a new formation stage until it is finally ready to be born. In the ninth month, the mother cheerfully receives her baby in her arms. If for any reason, the baby arrives before the nine months, it is considered premature and risks entering into the world with deformities or, even worse, facing death. Waiting is therefore crucial, that time is essential for developing everything necessary for a healthy end.

For many people, the word WAIT means to take a seat and do nothing at all. For them, it is to be still and without any movement. That's not necessarily the case. Waiting requires some action in order to prepare the atmosphere for the fulfillment of what is to come. Your efforts will develop all the necessary phases so that you may have a strong and healthy baby at the time of giving birth. In my case, my waiting period was preparing me to bring a dream into this world and to fulfill the vocation of becoming an evangelist. The Bible says:

"But those who WAIT on the Lord, shall renew their strength. They shall mount up with wings like eagles. They shall run and not be weary, They shall walk and not faint."
(Isaiah 40:31, NKJV)

"Wait for the Lord; be strong and take heart and wait for the Lord."
(Psalm 27:14, NIV)

In the book of Isaiah, the Word of God paints a picture for us of the quality of life that will result in those who learn to wait on the Lord. They will regain so much energy that their range and tolerance level will be out of the ordinary. "They shall run and not get weary; they shall walk and not grow weary." Yet in Psalm 27, we learn about the responsibility of those who wait on the Lord. Within that verse, we find two key directives, "be strong" and "take heart,"; both describing actions. "Be strong" means adding energy in the middle of difficulty. God often calls us to go against the grain, and this requires sacrifice. Don't give up; keep moving. "Take heart" involves provoking our own will in the face of discouragement. This action has everything to do with your attitude. Discouragement will come from the enemy and sometimes even from those we love. When no one else believes in what God has revealed to you, you have to learn to encourage yourself. Trust in the Lord, and while your dream is on its way to fulfillment, take steps of preparation. Then, when the moment of realization arrives, you can avoid failure due to a lack of preparedness, enabling the completion of a healthy dream.

As soon as my dream of being an evangelist was publicly confirmed by God, my father began to help me take steps towards preparation. Now instead of training me to box, he was engaging me to be an evangelist. When Christmas came around, my parents gifted me a karaoke machine to educate me on how to speak into a microphone. I have always said that my father has the art of preaching. Those who know him well, say the same. "Having the art" means to be capable of conveying to others the ability to understand and appreciate a message, even if they have no biblical knowledge. The exponent manages to transport you with such mastery until you experience everything he is communicating.

Beside my father, I learned to stand before an audience and convey my message. To know the difference between how and when I should raise my voice. He also instructed me on expressing myself with authority, speaking with the assurance that what I am saying is true. Above all, he has enabled me always to remember that we have a divine task in which all glory belongs to God. That the more God uses us, the humbler we need to be. I also learned that we must continually show compassion to people. What is the use of being an outstanding preacher, saving souls for the Kingdom of Christ, if my soul is lost in the end? Finally, he showed me that ministry is not a luxury but a great responsibility.

At that early age, I began visiting nursing homes and hospitals to pray for the sick. Every Thursday, my dad and I would drop by a chapel full of senior citizens, where I would preach and then pray for them, one by one. After ministering to them, we made our way into the rooms of every person confined to their beds, therefore unable to reach the chapel. We also preached in the street. My father preached in Spanish, and I translated the message to English. He became my role model. I imitated him in every way. At that point in my life, God had already changed many things in my father. I have learned it is always important to do good. Especially as we do not know whom we inspire and what message we send to those tiny eyes watching us.

I am a faithful believer that the most heard messages are not preached from a microphone. Rather, they occur when the microphone is turned off. Daddy became my hero and my best friend. Out of everyone who supported my dream, my father was the one who believed in me the most and the one who helped me above any other. As soon as God confirmed my calling through the Prophet Carlos Ramírez Jr., he became activated as my spiritual coach.

In my school, I was always an exemplary student. My teachers loved me. At the end of the school year, each teacher would say farewell to me with a hug and kiss. They always told my mother how they would miss me. I was a child who always behaved well in the classroom and therefore received privileges, including being the teacher's mailman. In those days, when texting was non-existent, if my teacher needed to send a message to another teacher or the principal, I was always the one chosen to be her postman. My responsibility was to carry the letter and its message from our classroom to the intended person. Then I had to wait for a response to deliver the answer to my teacher. I speak of this because, on one of the days when I was selected to carry a letter, my life was marked.

At this stage, I was 11 years old and already experienced the baptism of the Holy Spirit. It's true, at such a young age, I danced in the Spirit and spoke angelic tongues. When I felt the Glory of God, I would jump and run everywhere. In today's world, many are afraid of this act that often occurs in our evangelical churches. Some say we are crazy and full of sheer emotion. The reality is that the Bible speaks of this; it calls it "filling of the Spirit," or rather "empowerment."

The Bible says:

"But you shall receive power when the Holy Spirit has come upon you; and you shall be witnesses to Me in Jerusalem, and in all Judea and Samaria, and to the end of the earth."

(Acts 1:8, NKJV)

In other words, the Holy Spirit gives you the

necessary power so that you can be a witness to the Power of God on earth. The act of speaking in strange tongues or jumping whenever we feel the Spirit only indicates that something supernatural is upon us. As a child, I could understand that I would never be an authentic witness to the power of God on earth without that power. In my case, preaching His Word and praying for the healing of the sick would be ineffective without that empowerment. So this became one of my main requests. I came before God to tell him: "If I'm going to be an evangelist, I need the baptism of the Holy Spirit." Shortly after I asked for it, God granted it to me.

As I was saying, my teacher selected me to take a letter to the school principal. My classroom was on the third floor, and I had to walk to the end of the hall to go down the stairs into the first floor, where the principal's office was. Just as I was reaching the doors of the stairs, the Spirit of God came upon me. I started to dance and speak in tongues, but no one heard me. It was a divine moment of God.

As the Holy Spirit took me, He led me in front of a classroom. I noticed that the door was open, but the lights were off. Then, I heard the voice of God that said to me:

"Come in." Upon entering, I saw a teacher at her desk. There were no students in her classroom. She was alone, crying and writing on a piece of paper. It was there that I heard the voice of God telling me: "Tell her that although her husband abandoned her, I, Jehovah, have not abandoned her. She should not listen to that voice telling her: "take your life". At 11 years old, I had no knowledge of what a marriage was, but I was sure that the Spirit of God had sent me to that place, and I was only repeating what I heard from God.

That teacher had written a letter in which she said goodbye to the world on account of her decision to kill herself. In that letter, she tried to explain why she was going to commit suicide. As soon as I shared the words God had given me for her, her eyes went blank, and her voice changed. With an awful voice that caused fear and fright, she told me: "NO! I'LL TAKE HER TO HELL!" This was the first time I found myself in a situation like this. Never before had I faced a demon-possessed person. But the authority of the Holy Spirit took control of me, and I shouted: "Demon, release her now, in the Name of Jesus!" The demon within her cried out, and then the teacher fell from her chair to the ground. I ran to her. Putting my hand on her head, I prayed she would be okay. All of a sudden, she opened her eyes and asked: "What happened to me?" I replied: "God sent me to this place because He does not want you to take your life. God loves you". That teacher began to cry, questioning how I might have known that she wanted to end her life.

I introduced the plan of salvation to her, and she accepted Jesus. From that day until graduation, for the following two years, my recess time changed. Instead of going outside to play with the other children, daily, I met her in the classroom. There we prayed and read the Bible together. In the end, this teacher visited the church with me.

Later, God restored their marriage. On my graduation day, she told my mother how God had used me to save her life and how she got to know Jesus through me. That teacher hugged me tightly and said a few words that remained engraved in my heart. She told me, "Someday, I'll turn on my television and watch you preaching. You are destined for great things. You will carry the message of Jesus around the world." And you know what?

I believed her ...

Chapter 5

Divine Healing

I was never the type of person who waits for a crusade to exercise his calling. At the age of 11, I became the president of the children's ministry and a church musician. I played all the percussion instruments and the trumpet. In me, there was a yearning and a passion for everything that had to do with God. Every time I did something in service to God, I felt like I was getting closer each day to God's dream for my life. I always tended to act much older than I was. At 11 years old, I spoke as if I were 20. Generally, I was surrounded by young people and adults. They were my friends, I chatted with them, and they also enjoyed talking to me. People often came to my house looking for me. Sometimes when they rang the bell, it was to ask my parents if they would allow me to pray for them.

My pastor Ramón Luis Hernández, whom we considered our foster grandfather, was a man with an excessively strong character. I remember the many times when he allowed me to preach, and no matter how good my sermon was, he told me that I didn't know what I was talking about; that my preaching made no sense. However, many people would arrive crying at the altar, asking to receive Jesus as their Savior. His words repeatedly brought me to tears and crushed my spirit. By the time I reached my home, I would break down in my room questioning God in my prayers on whether He had really called me.

Just imagine having the feeling of absolute success when suddenly someone invades you, ruining your whole sense of accomplishment by insisting that you were not as successful as you imagined. But even so, I continued to believe and prepare for my calling. Before he died, my foster grandfather revealed why he said those things to me. He affirmed that I did know what I was saying. For my age, I understood more than some adults. He explained that I had a divine call from God, and due to the gift that I had received, he did not want me to be prideful. He taught me that the primary weapon in the destruction of every man is a prideful spirit. His job was always to keep me humble and straightforward because the day I gave way to pride, I would fall from the place where God had raised me. My grandfather was aware that his words perhaps saddened me, and for that, he asked me for forgiveness.

Furthermore, he told me that he was certain that nothing he could say to me would cause me to stop pursuing my dream. On the contrary, it would motivate me to be better. And so it was, I would enter my room, and although I cried, later I shook myself and prayed with more fervor. I started fasting and preparing myself even further in the Word.

I was a huge fan of evangelists like Yiye Ávila, Héctor de La Cruz, Carlos Ramírez Jr, Billy Graham and Rod Parsley. They were my role models and my inspirations. When I saw them on my television, I imagined I was like them. I owned a collection of all their videos and would wake up early on Sunday mornings to see Pastor Rod Parsley's show on TV. I imitated them every chance I could I get. I imitated them at every opportunity. I was preaching, even though I was the only one in my room with no audience whatsoever. Sometimes, even in the shower, I would preach. My mother would knock on the bathroom door and tell me: "It's time to make the altar call; there are others who also have to shower." On many occasions, I would go to clean the church with my dad. When we finished, I would climb the pulpit and started preaching. My dad supported me, listened to me, and then corrected me. He helped me to perfect my sermons.

Often, I read "Divine Healing," a book written by the evangelist Yiye Ávila. Through that book, I learned about miracles. Praying for the sick has always been my passion. I was endlessly fascinated by the possibility of witnessing creative miracles. I learned to have faith and to ask for the impossible. Faith is the key to every miracle and the channel of authority by which we declare things done, but only through the Name of Jesus.

Jesús said:

"And these signs will follow those who believe: In My name they will cast out demons; they will speak with new tongues; they will take up serpents; and if they drink anything deadly, it will by no means hurt them; they will lay hands on the sick, and they will recover."
(Mark 16:17-18, NKJV)

In the summer of 1997, my grandfather, moved by God, invited me to preach. Except that this time it was not inside the church. Instead, it was in the parking lot, outdoors, with a broad platform, just like in the Yiye Avila and Billy Graham campaigns. I could not believe it. The opportunity I wanted throughout my life was now before me. I prayed and fasted like never before. This time, I determined to preach as I had dreamed. For others, this might have been a standard service; however, it was the fulfillment of a dream for me. Even with all my enthusiasm, I could not know that this was the beginning of something powerful in my life. This occasion would clearly define a before and after in my history. The day came, August 14, 1997. I climbed onto the platform, which covered a large part of our church parking lot, Getsemani, in Newark, NJ. My legs were shaking, and my heart was pounding. As the audience arrived and settled outside in their chairs, I was inside the temple praying at the altar. I confess that today, even as an adult, my legs still shake. I still feel my heart rate accelerating because the power does not belong to me; this power is the power of God. I'm not the one who heals people; God is operating through my hands. He is the one who heals. I depend on Him, solely on Him.

I appeared on stage just in the nick of time to preach. In front of that vast crowd, I closed my eyes and dedicated myself to God. I preached under the theme "Divine Healing." My message lasted about 25 minutes, and as soon as I finished my sermon, people began to run to the stage. Some wanted to accept Jesus, and others needed a miracle. My grandfather grabbed the microphone and spoke to the crowd. He told them that God had given him specific instructions to anoint me as an evangelist on that night. Before I could pray for the people, I first needed to be anointed into the office of an evangelist. My parents joined me on the platform, and my grandfather holding the anointing oil said: "Rafael Cuevas Jr, today, August 14, 1997, as an ordained minister of God, I anoint you into the office of an evangelist. I set you apart for the ministry, so that you may preach the Word of God throughout the nations, with the sole purpose of bringing many lives to Jesus, and so that as you pray for the sick, and they are healed". At that moment, he began pouring the oil on my head while he said the following words: "The Spirit of the Lord is upon you." Immediately, I sensed that something supernatural flowed down my head, gravitating through my legs. As it descended on me, I danced and spoke in tongues. Simultaneously, all those who witnessed that beautiful moment also spoke in tongues and danced. Others were crying. It was a divine confirmation that heaven had set me apart for a sacred work on earth.

That night, after so many tears and hugs, I came home thanking God. I sensed something entirely different in my spirit. Something beautiful but indescribable. I was sure that my life would never be the same. I now have an immense responsibility on my shoulders. At the same time, I felt honored as God, the Father, had chosen me to carry out the privilege of bringing His Word to the world.

After a few days in prayer, someone asked me what the name of the ministry would be. "Divine Healing," I replied. From that moment, I began to carry a message of Faith and hope to the world. Through the name Divine Healing, I declared that through Faith in Jesus, everything is possible. The time for miracles had not yet expired. Wherever God guided me to preach His Word, miracles occurred. I was merely 11 years old when I began to travel with my parents. Whenever my preaching engagement was close to my church, the whole church would gather to support me in the event.

I know what it's like to go to events with more than 100 people after you. To see crowds getting off large buses, only to enter the places where it was your turn to preach. People named me "the preacher boy." I heard them as they declared with confidence that I carried something special from God. Some people even testified of the moment when I would grab the microphone. They said of me; this child changed completely. It was God himself ministering. A kid of that age is unable to flow with this kind of anointing and in that dimension.

I lived extremely passionate about preaching. I was never ashamed of my calling, much less of my Savior, Jesus. If we are ashamed of Him on earth, He will be ashamed of us before His Father. But if we honor Him on earth, in heaven He will honor us before His Father.

"For whoever is ashamed of Me and My words in this adulterous and sinful generation, of him the Son of Man also will be ashamed when He comes in the glory of His Father with the holy angels."
(Mark 8:38, NKJV)

I say this because even in school, I preached. My theory was that if those who sell drugs are not ashamed of what they do, why should I be ashamed of something that liberates people? When I entered High School, I became part of our school's Gospel Choir. A "sudden" Godly instance occurred during one of our school performances in front of 850 students. There are moments in life that will only happen once. Opportunities that present themselves for you to realize your dream. Some doors open to you; others you have to break down. In the middle of the concert, something or someone turned off the choir director's piano. After 30 minutes of worship, the music stopped. The director desperately sought to fix the problem as all the students started yelling and making fun of us. You can imagine the shame we were all beginning to feel.

The only things that still worked were the microphones. In this despair, three minutes had passed, and the students were agitated. As much as the teachers asked them to be quiet, they wouldn't stop. The choir director looked at me and said: "Rafael! Preach!" With much fear, I replied: "What! Here? Now?" "Yes," he responded. "Take the mic and preach until we fix this problem." You can probably imagine the nerves I experienced just at the thought of everyone making fun of my message. Above all, I wondered what to say to these 850 students since I was not in a church but in a school theater.

But then, I heard the voice of God saying with authority: "This is what I called you for." Suddenly I was filled with courage and grabbed the microphone. "I am Rafael Cuevas Jr, and today I have a message from heaven." Everyone in the theater became silent and curious to hear this message from above. "Today, I have come to speak to you not of a single religion but of a relationship. On this day, our friends came together to offer you a concert, but in reality, we are worshiping Jesus right in front of you. My fellow classmates, Jesus is the Son of God sent into the world so that we could all be saved. Through Him, our sins are forgiven, and we receive the guarantee of eternal life."

I continued saying: "The truth is many of you, right here in this place, are living with the appearance that everything is fine, while there is an immense void in your heart. To fill the emptiness of your soul, you run towards cigarettes, marijuana, or alcohol. You give yourself to your boyfriend or girlfriend. You join a gang or aim to be part of the most popular group at school. But today, Jesus is here to set you free, to heal your wounds. Just as many of you are not ashamed of smoking or fornicating, I am not ashamed of the gospel because it is the power of God. Jesus wants to fill your emptiness. He says: 'Come to me, all you who are weary and burdened, and I will give you rest' (Matthew 11:28, NIV). God has given us a gift called the Holy Spirit, whom we mentioned in our songs today. He is more than jumping and screaming. He is a Divine power. He is comfort. He is a friend. He is a brother. He is a Father. He is a Mother. Today Jesus wants you to walk out of this place with Him because 'if the Son sets you free, you will be truly free'" (John 8:36, NLT).

While saying those words, I began to notice that the teachers were crying. The students, including the school principal, were crying too. Some young people trembled and said their body hair was standing up. The Holy Spirit was touching them. When I delivered the altar call, many took to the stage. Others simply raised their hands, but they all listened to the message preached to them. Everyone paid attention with great respect. At the end of the message, as soon as the repentance prayer began, the piano started to function again. The choir initiated their song, and that is how we conclude the concert. I spent my High School years traveling on the weekends, preaching in many places. On Mondays, I arrived, just in time, to start the week of classes. It was my life until I finished High School. The teachers and my classmates called me: Reverend. They were highly supportive of my call, for that day, when I preached to them, God planted favor and grace for me.

I preached the message that I was passionate about, Divine Healing. On my travels, I prayed for the sick, and God healed them in front of everyone. Week after week, miracles took place before my eyes, but I had never experienced a miracle myself. I have always been a healthy boy. But I ask you, how can one speak with authority about a Jesus who heals the sick if you have never been ill? If you have never received a miracle of healing, how can you describe to others the process of trusting in Jesus, who lifts and restores? Whoever feels like he has never fallen and never lost anything can never understand the fullness of God's grace.

Everything was about to change. It is not the same to preach on another's experience as it is to preach on oneself. My life was on the verge of a sharp and violent turn. I was just about to find out what I was really made of. Was I truly an evangelist? Or was I merely a copy of something I saw on television? The upcoming test for my life was about to reveal all this and much more.

Chapter 6

This Is Not What I Dreamt

During my high school years, my parents began to pastor a small congregation that soon grew at a remarkable speed. As I mentioned a few chapters ago, my father has the art of preaching. Many people came to hear him speak. The church location was in one of the most dangerous places in Newark, NJ. Crime and drug sales were abounding, but God sent us there. I must confess, at first, my sisters and I were terrified to be in that place. However, within a few months of starting the ministry, we noticed a massive change in that neighborhood. Every time my dad preached, people flocked to the front of the church to listen to him. My dad easily won the affection of people. Even drug traffickers asked him for prayer and decided to pause drug sales during service hours. In fact, they moved their drug business to another street.

In his third year as pastor, my father began suffering from high blood pressure. He took to heart the many severe problems of the congregation, and this affected his health. At 16, I began to live what I once believed to be impossible; my father slipped into severe spiritual neglect and returned to a life of drugs. After so many years without using heroin! After living a life free of that monster! Once again, my dad was addicted to drugs.

I was fully in the process of ministerial development, still attending high school and traveling every weekend to preach. As this happened, my father left his office as a pastor, and my heart broke. I could not understand how the man who had taught me the Word of God had returned to drugs. What could have driven his return to that evil world? I was suffering from the loss of my hero. I felt as if every bit of innocence was literally ripped away from me. I was left abandoned and betrayed. He was my best friend, my traveling companion, my armor-bearer, my protector, my coordinator, and my teacher. And now he was gone; the drugs took possession of him. Trust me when I say we did everything to help him, but nothing worked. We isolated ourselves at home, so he could break that vice in cold blood, as they say. Watching my father jump on the bed, shivering in pure summer, so cold as if the house were frozen, is an experience that will remain in the depths of my heart forever. I became a human blanket so that his body would warm and not shiver from the cold. We found ourselves forced to take him constantly to the bathroom. If he wasn't vomiting, we had to bathe him since the water served as a pain reliever. In that state, he lost all control of his bodily functions and even soiled himself. But shortly after breaking that vice, he returned to drugs.

From the age of 16, I had to take care of my home. At that early age, I had to help my mother in every way I could. Forced to trade in being a young man for becoming a man, on my shoulders, I carried an enormous responsibility that, in reality, did not correspond to me.

It seemed like I was living in a bad dream. Now I realize that in order for my dream to come true, I first had to live a complete nightmare.

Nothing was the same... Everything changed. That happy home became an unhappy one, just as it once was at the beginning. Birthdays were never the same again. The grand Christmas celebrations also stopped occurring. Nevertheless, I did my best to celebrate birthdays, Christmas and to make sure we had a turkey at home on Thanksgiving Day. My younger sister, Fanny, was barely 12 years old; she was my biggest concern. I did everything I could to make sure she never lacked anything. My mother remained as the church pastor in my father's place, but many people left. Again, it was not the same. I started traveling without my dad, and in those days, I found the true definition of loneliness and abandonment. I managed to preach in many places without him. And since he was no longer with me, they often kept the offering money that the congregation raised for me.

In my city, within the Christian community, I was rejected by the people. I felt as if I was paying for the sin of another. When my father fell into drugs, many churches stopped accepting me as a preacher. They treated me as if I were the addict. Despite everything, I came to many events, not as a preacher but to show my support. There they publicly greeted the ministers, young and old, all except me. They allowed the participation of every minister who attended the event; I was the only exception. People said that I would be the next to fall, and soon they would see me on a street corner selling or using drugs. But this is where I discovered that I do not depend on my earthly father but my Heavenly Father.

My relationship with Jesus helped me stay focused on the call and continue to pursue the dream of being an evangelist. Above all, I did not serve God because I had a calling but because I loved Him. I was determined; nothing was going to separate me from Jesus. In those trying moments, I needed Him more than any other time in my life. Since they refused to receive me in many places within my city, God began to take me much further. In this case, the common saying applies, originated by Jesus himself, which says that no one is a prophet in his own land. (see Luke 4:24) My mother managed to travel with me to several places. Because I was a minor, someone had to accompany me on every trip. After graduating from school, I continued to travel without the supervision of an adult.

As I boarded many airplanes, I cried as if I was on my way to a funeral rather than a crusade. I needed my dad. I enjoyed historic moments with God in those crusades, but I had no one with whom to celebrate what God was doing. There were moments when the Glory of God came down on the people, and God healed the sick; supernatural events took place. At times like these, I could not contain the tears, and they began pouring out. However, I wasn't crying because I joined them under the manifested glory, but because I missed my dad. I pictured myself as an orphan child.

He and I had so many conversations about the crusades. We anticipated that one day we would get to live them together. And here I was, reaching those dreams, without my dad. I carried an incredible pain in my heart. Everybody would leave my crusades joyful and free, but I came home saddened, wondering where my dad would be. Many times he would disappear and leave us worried without the slightest idea of where he might be. So I couldn't even tell him about my experience during the crusade.

I managed to have great crusades like the one in Turks and Caicos in 2003, where more than a thousand people gathered at a ballpark to celebrate Jesus. There, I saw witches accepting Jesus as their Savior, and God healed hundreds of people. Crusades like the one in 2004, in Puerto Plata, where it began to rain on the basketball court in front of a thousand people. In the middle of my sermon, I stood up with authority and said, "Rain, Stop in Jesus' Name!" Instantly, in front of the whole town, it stopped raining. One can imagine how the Glory of God was poured out in that place, as the people became witnesses of that even heavy rain has no choice but to obey the power of God.

With all this, and even after these glorious demonstrations, whenever I came home, I encountered chaos due to my father's condition. He showed up at our house and stole everything he found from us. And if it weren't that, someone would knock on the door of the house, collecting some money that my father had borrowed from them. Sometimes we got calls from prison where he cried and pleaded for me to get him out. I no longer found peace because the one place where I was supposed to obtain my rest after momentous events had become a living hell. I didn't even have the ease to fast at home. At the same time, when my father wasn't keeping us in some kind of trouble, my mother was fighting with him due to the awful life he was leading. I don't blame her, for we are only human, and the burden was too great. She came to believe that with her hands, she would change him. I remember those nights when I was awakened from my sleep because she was breaking something on his head, she was throwing all his clothes out the door, or she was using my dad's head to create another hole in the wall.

When the particulars mentioned above would happen in pure winter, it broke my heart to see the face of my father, who sadly picked up his clothes amid so much cold. At midnight, as I watched him take the street with that eerie frostiness, I would get dressed and get in my car to look for him. Then I waited until my mother fell asleep to sneak him into the house, so he wouldn't have to sleep outside in the cold. Fanny and I gave him food saying: "You have to go before Mom gets up in the morning." When dawn came, before we woke up, he would leave and come back at night.

The cycle continued; I would open the door for him, feed him, and then he would leave in the morning. We got to do this many times, especially during winter.

There were times when I would take him to a detox clinic where they cleaned his blood. After leaving that place, he lasted up to 30 days without using drugs. He would spend at least a month clean, without any drug use, yet he would go looking for drugs again as soon as he had any quarrel with my mother. My older sister, Yajaira, no longer wanted to live in that type of environment, so she moved out of the house as soon as possible. I can't blame her. She was already a grown high school graduate striving to pursue her career. To avoid the frequency of incidents and avoid time at home, I accepted all possible invitations for each event or crusade. From wherever I was, I would send money to my mom and my sister. Sometimes, I managed to spend up to three months outside my house. I often preached far away, so I didn't have to deal with the hell in which I lived.

I began to get frustrated as I watched many people finding freedom whenever I preached to crowds, but I could not free my father. On one occasion, I even said, "God, I will not preach your Word again, because how is it that miracles happen when I preach and lives are transformed, yet my father continues to be an addict"? And He answered me: "Because your job is to preach and mine is to transform." The reality is God cannot change or transform someone unless the person allows it.

After some time living like this, I was already tired of my life. Watching a dream come true while experiencing hell at home prevented it from seeming like a dream at all. With each trip, the loneliness and abandonment only grew. I felt like I didn't have parents. After all, they only called me whenever there was a problem. No one cared to know if I had arrived safely at my destination, whether I had eaten, or if I was treated well in the places where I was preaching. Many times I boarded the plane without even a penny for a soda. I would leave all my money at home so that my family could eat; therefore, I had to wait to get on the plane to eat or drink the airline's complimentary food. With every trip, the burden increased. I knew that as soon as I returned from a glorious victory, the enemy would be waiting for me at home. Whenever I returned to the city of Newark, NJ, I sensed depression greeting me at the airport. It was as if she greeted me and escorted me to my house. No one else would show up to greet me joyfully at the airport.

I was highly frustrated, so much so that I reached the

point where I said to God, "Take me." In December 2007, at the age of 22, I gazed out of an airplane window and told God how lonely I felt not having anyone to understand me. Also, I was utterly ashamed to be an evangelist and still have a home like mine. The reality was that although I took on the office of the priesthood, this was not my home; it belonged to my parents. Through their bad decisions, both had created a harmful environment that robbed us of the possibility of living in peace.

There are frustrations in life that arise because we are assuming responsibilities that do not correspond to us. In my case, I became the priest of my home when it was my father's responsibility, not mine. My role was to be the son, but circumstances forced me to take the wheel since everything was going downhill. I never imagined that God would allow all this to form in me, the man I am today. Sometimes Jesus does not rebuke the winds in our lives because they are responsible for teaching us how to walk through the storm. To live as someone who finds peace in the midst of the storm.

Even though I was staring out of an airplane window, telling God to "take me," it doesn't mean I was thinking about suicide. Only God gives us life, and only God can take it away. I do not believe in suicide, and for those who carry out such acts, heaven will certainly not wait for them. At that time, I was negotiating with God, saying that for my age, I had already achieved a lot in the gospel, or at least that was what I believed. At the age of 22, even though I considered myself very successful in my calling, I now understand that God's thoughts will always be higher than ours.

During that year, I began to feel discomfort in my left knee. Sometimes I felt a lot of irritation and even pain, but I didn't care to see a doctor. During my last tour in 2007, I went to preach to the state of Florida on a crusade that would go from Orlando to Tampa, Fl. During my prayer time, the Spirit of God spoke to me, saying: "Prepare to face cancer." I understood that this disease, which in many events led me to pray and watch God healing so many, would now touch my life. I replied to God: "If this is the way you will take me, I am happy because I know that I have done Your will and that I have lived for You."

Life has a saying that says: "It is not the same to call the enemy than to see him come." I had heard this many times, but I was about to find out what it truly meant. That saying was about to be materialized in me.

Chapter 7

As I See It Coming

My family was a ministerial one. My dad possessed the gift of preaching, and at the same time, he was an excellent teacher of the Word, who carried an impressive manifestation of God. My mother had the gift of working with children. At the beginning of her ministry in the church, she became the leader of more than fifty children. She managed this department on her own. My mother would go throughout the streets asking the neighboring parents' permission to bring their children to the church. She convinced them to have them join a weekly group where children carried out biblical stories through plays. Both of my sisters dominated the gift of praise and worship. Whenever they sing, heaven touches the earth. I believe with all my heart that the enemy was so fierce in destroying our home for that reason.

The enemy does not attack people who are no threat to him. What's more, I dare to say that he is not afraid of who you are today; rather, he is terrified of what you can become tomorrow. The war in my house was too aggressive, and I was drained. Every time I went on a crusade, I found things worse by the time I came back. Returning to what I recently revealed: "I was wearing myself emotionally." I managed to exhaust all my strength in an attempt to fulfill my duty as a son, as well as all the responsibilities that belonged to my parents.

I remember hearing my dad speaking regularly about his father during his first few sermons. He shared about their great friendship, even though a spirit of alcoholism tormented his father. From time to time, his dad took to alcohol, and despite having children, a wife, and a pleasant home, he acted like a homeless man on the street. My dad would describe the many times that this spirit took control and how whenever his father indulged in alcohol, he would spend days without returning home. So, my dad would go out looking for him. Every time he found him, he brought him home. There he bathed him, shaved him, and gave him a trim. He put clean clothes on him and kissed him. He hugged him and told him that he loved him. For a short while, his dad was calm, avoiding even a drop of alcohol, but this resolve did not last long. Suddenly, the smell of liquor saturated the house, and simultaneously, his father would disappear.

The madness of all this is, I remember hearing that and then asking God never to allow me to experience something like this with my dad. The two greatest fears of my life were that my father would go back to drugs or that my parents would get divorced. I pleaded with God that neither of these two things would ever happen. After hearing my dad preaching those sermons about his father, I now found myself doing the same thing as him, searching for my father on all the streets. And whenever I found him, I would bring him home. There I bathed him, shaved him, and perfumed him. I prayed for him and kissed him. And I would say to him: "Now you look like the Pastor I know."

But the last straw was in November 2007, a month before God spoke to me about cancer. Once again, I found myself, on Thanksgiving Day, crying over my dad's absence. After making a big purchase to celebrate our dinner, my father was still missing when my mother served the turkey. I was able to say grace, but I could not eat. That week when I arrived from a crusade, my dad was on the streets. As soon as I got out of the plane, straight away, I went to search for him but couldn't find him. This caused a profound sadness in me. This holiday was a time to be with family, but mine was incomplete. Still, I continued with the preparations for dinner. Despite everything, I always wanted us to continue celebrating those special days in my house, just like Christmas and birthdays were.

While we were eating, the phone rang, and on the other end was my dad's voice. I was so happy to hear him. I said, "Dad, I'm waiting for you to arrive so that I can eat with you. Where are you"? In his reply, he stated that while he was hungry, he had no plans of coming home for dinner. When I asked where I could meet him, he replied, "at the gas station." I prepared a couple of plates of food, not only for him, but also for me. It was a cold day that day. When I reached the gas station, I found him sitting on the sidewalk in the parking lot. I got out of the car and sat next to him. I put my arm on him and asked for his blessing.

I took out the bag of food, and I handed him his plate. I also grabbed mine and started eating with him. He cried as he ate his dinner, urging me to go home. I assured him: "I asked God for an opportunity to eat with you today, and I'm not leaving here until we finish eating together. You are not alone in these streets. I am in the streets with you". At the end of the meal, I gave him some money. I begged him to come home with me, but he refused. With tears in my eyes, I got into my car while I watched him walk away until he disappeared.

I was suffering so much that when God told me that I would face cancer, I understood it as a way of Him saying to me: "This is where your mission on earth has come to an end. You will not suffer any more pain. You no longer have to live frustrated by your home life". The sad reality defined my ministry as a growing success, but my personal life was falling apart.

At the end of my last tour in 2007, I returned home to celebrate Christmas. As usual, I was already making arrangements to celebrate with my sisters and my mother. In Puerto Rico, during 2006, I believed I had injured my left knee while straining to lift a boat. Since then, between 2006 and 2007, I complained of significant pain in that knee. At first, I concluded it was nothing. As a minister who moves in the anointing of miracles, I would simply pray for the pain and then continue the crusades. By the end of 2007, the pain worsened. I was unaware that I had a cancerous tumor in my knee that was slowly eating away at the bones of my left leg. However, I ignored the pain to care for my family during Christmas. The next day the pain intensified, and my knee took the shape of a basketball.

If I could describe the pain to you, it was as if someone was stabbing me relentlessly with the biggest knife in the kitchen. It seemed to me that the pain increased with every second. I could no longer resist the torture and decided to visit the doctor. When he saw me, his words were: "You need to go to the hospital at once because this does not look good."

Apparently, he had a good idea of what was happening, as the concern on his face denounced it. They immediately transferred me to the emergency room, where they were waiting for me with a stretcher. My anxiety level increased, not so much from pain, but from watching the reaction of everyone who received me at the hospital. In their hastened treatment, I felt like a patient who shows up with a gunshot to the chest, and the entire hospital staff moves in to help him.

As I witnessed all that movement, I said to myself: "Nuni, this is ugly." The pains were so intense that I could no longer bear them, and I began to scream and cry in utter despair. I cried out and, at the same time, prayed that God would take away my pain. Amid the shouting, a nurse came in and gave me an injection. I noticed that the room began to spin round and round and round as if it would never stop.

I had been injected with what they considered the most potent form of morphine.

My body was not familiar with drugs. The only drug it knew of was called Tylenol. Getting that injection only caused me to feel dizzy, spinning quickly. My dad went crazy; he started fighting with the doctors and nurses. You see, as an addict, he had first-hand knowledge of the real damage that this drug could cause me. He began to cry, hoping that his son would not have to fight the same monsters he often faced. The doctors set my parents aside to explain that everything happening to me raised much concern. Although I had yet to be X-rayed or subjected to a CT SCAN, they gathered, from experience, that this was an extreme case.

The crazy thing about it is that I asked my mother to communicate with my sister Fanny because that night, I was scheduled to preach at an event in my city. After such a long time, they were finally allowing me to preach in my town. I had faith that I would quickly get out of the hospital, so I asked my sister to prepare my clothes for the event. When the doctor overheard our conversation, he said to me: "Mr. Cuevas, you are not leaving this hospital. So make yourself comfortable because you won't get up from here until we know what you have". At that moment, I understood that what God had previously revealed to me, I would soon hear from these doctors.

My relatives were all disturbed. They did not understand what was actually happening, but in my spirit, I knew it because God had already prepared me. As I said before, it is not the same to call the enemy than to see him come. Immediately I began to feel great sadness because I said: "I am leaving. My time has come". I thought of my sister Fanny, who at that moment was the most important thing to me. She was the youngest in the house at just 17 years old. I considered that I would leave her alone with that battle at home, without someone to watch over her. I thought of the pain my parents would feel at having to bury me, for no parent should ever have to bury their children.

After several days and several biopsies, the doctor came into my room and sat down on a chair to talk to me. As I watched this doctor lifting the chair and placing it next to my bed to get closer to me, my heart turned to jelly. I could not contain myself, my eyes began to water, and my body trembled with fear of what he might say to me. Even the doctor, without mentioning a word, was already crying. With great sadness, taking me by the hand, he said: "Mr.

Cuevas, the results of your exams are not good. You have bone cancer. The cancer was formed through a tumor in your knee. Since you have not been cared for before, it is in its fourth stage. It moves forward at an accelerated pace, devouring all the bones in your left leg. I'm sorry to tell you that in my experience you have approximately six months to live. "Crying inconsolably, that doctor hugged me and then left the room to allow me some time alone. I still remember hearing his footsteps, slowly retreating from that room. I detected the chill of death entering that place, and loneliness took hold of me. In anguish, I asked God, ¿Where did I fail him? Many people believe that if something terrible happens to us in life, we must have done something evil. That is a process of false thinking in people. It wasn't that I had done something bad but that I had done something good. Let me explain; my Faith in God led Him to trust me with a demanding test like cancer because He knew that someone else could not handle it. God knew that such a trial would not break me; instead, it would result in unleashing a greater Glory in me.

"For our light affliction, which is but for a moment, is working for us a far more exceeding and eternal weight of glory."
(2 Corinthians 4:17, NKJV)

Now that the doctor had shared his diagnosis, I was working on preparing myself, mentally and spiritually, for what was to come. I was trying to condition myself for revealing my diagnosis in an upcoming conversation with my parents and sisters. But above it all, God had a pending conversation for me ...

Chapter 8

You Should've Thought Bigger

Life did not allow me a brother, it only gave me two sisters, but it did provide me with Andrew. Andrew is my first cousin because his father and my father are brothers by blood. This means he also carries the surname Cuevas. Andrew is five years older than I. As children, his parents lived in Brooklyn, NY, so I only saw him during holidays in those days. His parents prepared huge banquets, and the whole family gathered at his house. There, we ate and sang praises to the Lord. I stopped seeing Andrew when his family moved to Kissimmee, Fl, when I was eight years old. But in 2001, God brought us together again, and this time to work together in the Kingdom of God.

During the last tour of 2007, when God told me that I would be diagnosed with cancer, I remember thinking that I would never see Andrew again after that trip. It was 6:00 am, and Andrew was placing my bags in the trunk of his mother's car. If anyone knew how I felt and the pain I carried inside, it was him. Andrew and I talked a lot; he always imparted much faith into my life and helped me believe in myself, even more than I thought. He was a handkerchief to my tears, the coach who took my dad's place—always ensuring that I did the right thing. I will never forget the look that he gave me the morning before heading home. There was pity in his eyes because he knew that I was unhappy in my home and how much more at peace I was during our tours. When God would speak to me, Andrew knew that things would come to pass, just as God told me. For that reason, I had not yet revealed what God told me. I didn't want to share such a thing, especially since we were about to celebrate Christmas.

So, before entering the car that would get us to the airport, I looked at him and smiled, even though with tears. I hugged him, saying, "Thank you for never leaving me and for all the support you have shown me. We have had a good time together. You are my brother and my blood, the brother I have always asked God for. I love you". I kissed his cheek with a slow and deliberate kiss because I did not want that moment to end. I assumed that this would be the last time we saw each other. Usually, he wouldn't let me kiss him because although I know he loves me, Andrew is not the type of person to show affection. Unlike him, I have always been an affectionate person. That morning he felt that something was wrong, so he let me kiss him on the cheek, and then he kissed mine and said, "I love you too. You are my brother". I boarded my flight and returned to New Jersey.

Andrew and I spoke on the phone at all hours. Our relationship goes beyond siblings and best friends; we have yet to find a name to describe our friendship. Every short while, we called each other for the most insignificant details, and we both made ourselves laugh. Our bond was so strong that cancer couldn't alter it, so from my hospital bed, we continued our conversations. Especially when I couldn't bear that pain, so severe that I felt like I would literally lose my mind. I would never have imagined an ache so intense that it would lead someone to lose their mind. Remember that in my case, I have always been a very healthy boy. I had never been to a hospital before. Andrew had told me that if I felt those pains, I should call him. So whenever that agony took hold in my leg, I immediately pressed the button to call the nurse, and in the time it took her to bring me the medication, I picked up the phone and called my brother Andrew. Shouting in pain, I would call him, and he would answer me immediately.

With a voice filled with agony, I would say to him:

"Andrew, I have pain. My God, I can't take it. Pray for me". Imagine, every time I experienced that pain, it was because some part of my bones was actually disappearing. So no matter what he was doing or what time it was, Andrew would drop everything to pray for me.

Sometimes he would play the guitar while we waited for the nurse to arrive with the medicine. He was my therapy. Every time we spoke, I felt far from the hospital. Sometimes when he played the guitar, he had his sister Debbie singing on the phone. Every night, with their songs, they made me feel close to God. Andrew was the first person with whom I shared what the doctor said. In order not to frighten him, I would tell him: "Apparently, they think that it could be that" while I already knew that it was cancer, with a prognosis of only six months to live. Since I was 22 years old, this meant I would not get to see my 23rd birthday..

2007 was coming to an end. It was New Year's Eve, and I was alone in that hospital room. As was customary, everyone was at the church altar, celebrating the new year. At 11: 45 p.m., I turned on my computer to listen to worship music. Closing my eyes, I began to worship God. I said, "Lord, forgive me if I have offended you in some way or if I have failed you in something. Thank you for the kind of life you have given me. I'm not going to fight with you. If you want to take me with cancer, Amen. So be it. Let Your will be done and not mine. I only ask that you strengthen me so that I can get through this trying time. I also ask You to strengthen my family. Today, I want to thank you. Thank you for choosing me to preach Your word. Thank you for standing by my side in that Bible school where I met you. Thank you for the lives that have come to your feet in the crusades. For all the miracles you did. Now I can understand why I started preaching at a young age because my time on earth would not be very long. So today, I give you the gift that you have given me. I'll give it back to you multiplied. I love you, Lord". With my hands raised, I continued to glorify God until I opened my eyes to see how much time was left until the arrival of 2008.

When I opened my eyes, I tried to look, but there was nothing. Also, I realized I was not lying on a bed; I was on my feet, but I still could not see anything. In that darkness, I experienced a lot of peace and no fear. I spoke and said, "Lord, where am I?" As I said those words, I heard the echo of my voice, which gave me the impression that I was in a large and spacious place, somewhere where I was alone, without anyone else. At that moment, I noticed a ray of light descending towards me, and when it touched me, the whole place filled with light. There was a golden stairway in front of me. I was thrilled, as I felt incredible peace along with utter joy like I had never known before. I began to hear breathtaking worship, a choir singing in unity: "HOLY, HOLY, HOLY." I could hear the song from a distance and yet, at the same time, nearby. The stairs were shining with great brilliance, and I could see snow-white clouds and golden gates at the top. In the distance and behind those gates, I noticed a beautiful city made of gold. I knew that I was at the doorway to Heaven.

With much enthusiasm, I started up the stairs, but suddenly, they began to tremble. I fell to my knees and lowered my face; somehow, I knew I was about to hear the voice of God. "Rafael Cuevas Jr., Nuni, it is not time for you to climb the stairs because I still have a lot to do with you." Immediately I opened my eyes. It was midnight, and I heard the voices of nurses and doctors saying, "Happy New Year!" 2008 had arrived. He could not believe what he had seen and what he had just heard from God. Then I heard again the voice of God that said to me: "YOU SHOULD'VE THOUGHT BIGGER."

Chapter 9

He Remembered Me

When God revealed His intention with this cancer, I understood I would not die, that something powerful was about to emerge. When God gives a word of hope, like the one He declared over me, it is like showing us a light at the end of a tunnel. Your darkness is not eternal. Something miraculous is going to happen. Think about it; God himself lets you know that there is a way out of your problem. What he often does not tell you is when and how the miracle will happen.

That when and how, makes the difference in determining what material you are made of. So Nuni was about to discover his own ingredients. I have always had great Faith in Jesus. Faith is like an exercise; the more you put it to work, the stronger you will be in it. I stand firm in the knowledge that "for those who believe nothing is impossible." Now, this statement doesn't work simply because you choose to believe. For your Faith to flourish, what matters most is who you believe in and why you believe. Since my childhood, there is a scripture that has always been the key to my trust in miracles. Jesus said, "All things are possible to him who believes" (Mark 9:23, ESV). Miracles happen whenever the impossible occurs. Jesus is the expert at making the impossible, possible.

There I was, believing God for a miracle in my personal life. My confidence was standing firm on the voice of God, which assured me that this miracle was part of His plan. So I began to declare that He would get me out of that bed and that the cancer would disappear. I was confident that at any moment, that basketball ball on my leg would disappear, and I would walk out of the hospital. And it wasn't that God wasn't able to do it that way, but His plan extended far beyond healing me from cancer.

Seeing that the cancer did not go away, I began to despair. I noticed that my leg kept getting worse, and the pain increased. I prayed and prayed and prayed, and nothing happened. Daily, instead of improving, my condition deteriorated to the point that I stopped walking altogether. My left leg lost all its strength, while the good leg was also affected, along with every other bone in my body. Every minute, the cancer was gaining ground, and another part of my bones was destroyed. The doctors' best recommendation for my family was to make the necessary arrangements since I would not last long.

Imagine sitting in a hospital room watching your family in search of a place to hold your funeral. They are also choosing your coffin, the flowers for the wake, and even in which church the services will be held. It was a heartbreaking scene. Even the notion of such an experience is one of the saddest thoughts that any young person can have. No matter how great my Faith was, the reality of the problem made me feel like I couldn't do enough. The disease seemed much larger than my portion of Faith. Still, to behold a miracle, I had to use whatever Faith remained. These moments are often designed in such a way that you can put all your Faith into practice.

The cancer was so advanced, the doctors did not want to operate on my leg to remove the tumor, nor did they want to provide me with chemotherapy treatment. According to the doctors, it was too late. The time for hopeful treatment had passed. It was supposed to be when I experienced my first symptoms. I should have visited a doctor in 2006, when I first felt discomfort in my knee. Still, I dare say that this was all part of God's plan. If I had visited them at the beginning of my discomfort, then the doctors and their treatments would receive all the glory. In this case, God, and only God, made sure that only He received the glory.

For this reason, I speak to those who are in a difficult situation today. Perhaps similar to mine, where no man can offer you a solution because you can't find a solution if people give up on you. To them I say: get ready! All it means is God is on the verge of taking over. God will do what no man can do so that no man can take credit for your miracle. You just have to put all your Faith in Jesus.

My family did not know how to react to the news. I remember telling my sister Yajaira and hearing her voice on the phone when she cried out: "NO, NOT YOU!" She considered me a good boy and couldn't understand why God allowed such a disease in my life. I was a vibrant young man with goals, a wonderful ministry, and a full life ahead of me. As I spoke to my sister, it was as if they were replaying a film of my whole life with her. She was my first friend. The memories of us playing hide-and-seek, sitting in front of the TV watching our favorite shows, or running around the yard looking for ants, suddenly rushed in. I could also remember the tiny pool in which our parents put us in whenever summer arrived and how we shared the same bed at night when we were afraid.

I still remember seeing my little sister Fanny's face, full of pain and great concern. I took her by the hand on my hospital bed and said: "Easy, Fanny, I'm going to fight until God heals me." And she told me: "And I'm going to fight next to you. I will not leave you alone". And so she did, she even left the university to tend to me. She became my personal nurse. Nevertheless, the days passed, and God did not say anything to me, and my level of pain continued to rise. What do you do when you pray, and God does not answer you? The answer is simple: Keep believing. Keep praying. Do everything except give up.

So I said to God in prayer: "I have never served you for what you can give me. If you heal me, we are friends, and if you do not heal me, we will continue to be friends. I will always serve You. But there's one thing that I must ask: "Why have you forgotten me? At this moment, I feel like You abandoned me, for whenever I pray, You don't answer me, nor show me any improvement." While I was making that prayer in my mind, Mrs. Oliver entered my hospital room. "Mrs. O," as we affectionately call her, is an African-American minister with a beautiful track record in the gospel. Long before I was born, she was a singer in her church choir and participated in various music recordings. At that time, she was also known as a renowned preacher.

I grew up asking her blessing because she was my neighbor for many years. She was an absolute blessing for my family and our community. Dressed in her minister's clothes, she appeared with a black shirt and white collar and carried the anointed oil in her hand. Her greeting was: "My son, I have not forgotten you! This disease is not unto death. It is for you to behold my Glory". I knew that God was speaking to me through her. Immediately I felt God's impact in my heart, and the tears began to flow down my face.

Then she poured the oil into her hands and began anointing my leg, saying: "Illness, you have no part or chance in this body. This body belongs to God, and you must leave, in the Name of Jesus." Indeed, God was visiting me through His servant. I was weeping and thanking God for this special encounter. "Mrs. O" anointed my head and said: "Today, I anoint you for the war that you will have to face. In all this, always be sure to proclaim that you are healthy, do not stop believing, and do not give room to doubt. Don't say that God has forgotten you. From this, God will receive the Glory. And when you get out of this process, the Glory of your ministry will be greater than the first. She anointed my ears as he said, "I am anointing your ears to hear what God has to say to you at this time." She anointed my mouth and told me: "I am anointing your mouth so that you speak with anointing all that God will show you in this time of illness." And so she ended the prayer.

I entrusted my life into the hands of God, thanking Him for answering my prayer. I expressed my deepest gratitude for the miracle He was going to perform and the strength that only He could give me in this time of trouble. I began to declare that my time had not come to leave this earth. That God was in control. I did not know how or when the miracle would happen, but I was sure that God was going to do it. I tried my best not to get carried away by the pain I was experiencing, nor by the fact that I could no longer walk. Rather, I became focused entirely on what God was going to do.

Chapter 10

The Doctor of All Doctors

Prayer is the key to a connection with God. It's the phone line that puts you in touch with His heavenly throne. Jesus, it's the signal tower that connects your call. The Bible records the words of Jesus as He stated: "I am the way, the truth, and the life, and no one comes to the Father except through me" (John 14:6, ESV). For this reason, from my childhood, every time I pray, I begin my prayer by saying: "Father, in the name of Jesus." I believe in this prayer method because I have seen many favorable results while praying in this way. Jesus also said: "And whatever you ask in my name, I will do it so that the Father may be glorified in His Son" (John 14:13, NIV).

I say all this to tell you about what happened after Mrs. O's visit. During difficult times, like I was living, it is easy to discover who your true friends are. When I think back to my battle with cancer, there are two kinds of people who stand out; those who abandoned me and those who stood in the gap for me. Among the faithful is a friend by the name of David Ramos. David was a youth leader. Every Monday, David and his youth group gathered for prayer meetings at the temple. After their prayer time, they would spend some time in worship, and then David culminated with a word. I had the opportunity to attend several of their meetings and the honor to preach at some of them. I missed being there because every time I went, I left with new strength. Until further notice, I could not join them since I was hospitalized, but David always reached out to me. He would visit me with his Bible in hand and with a word that would lift my spirits. His visit never failed. One Monday, after saying goodbye to all my visitors, I was left alone in my hospital room. I was meditating in silence and talking to God when my cell phone rings suddenly. David and his youth group were online. As usual, they were meeting in the temple, but this time everyone was standing in the gap for me.

They began to speak words of encouragement to me. To proclaim that cancer would not kill me. Around 50 young people cried out to God for my health with audible passion. Every prayer was canceling the doctor's prognosis. I couldn't understand exactly what each individual was saying, as they were all praying simultaneously, but I knew the cancer was in trouble. Jesus said: "Furthermore, I tell you that if two of you agree on anything you ask here on earth, it will be done for you by My Father who is in heaven" (Matthew 18:19, NASB).

For several minutes, they interceded for me, pleading and crying out loud. I also connected with them in the spirit. As we prayed together, I started noticing that there was interference on the line, and I could barely hear the young people praying for me. While I was listening to interference, I also noticed the smell of anointed oil all over my room. The smell of oil had a unique flowery scent. The more I detected the flower and oil combination, the more the call was disconnected until I could no longer hear the young people praying. I felt a supernatural peace entering my hospital room. At the entrance of my room, I observed a doctor knocking on the door and asking my permission to enter. When I allowed him to enter, I realized that I had never seen him before. His face was glowing, and he wore a beautiful smile.

As he drew closer, the smell of oil mixed with flowers grew. I marveled at the amount of shine on his white hair was. I've never seen such a thing. Dressed in a doctor's coat, he kept moving towards me, and it seemed like the world had stopped spinning for a few minutes. At that moment, no one else existed, just the two of us, him and I. Everything happened as if we were moving in slow motion. I was curious to know who he was, so I checked to learn the name written on his name tag. It read: Dr. Nazareth.

My mother had brought me a warm blanket from home, which I liked to use to sleep. It was my favorite blanket, and it made me feel comfortable. Those who know me know that I am a child inside the body of a man who is six feet tall. Imagine, my blanket had Spider-Man on it. When the doctor got close, he looked at me and said: "Rafael Cuevas, how are you feeling?" His voice gave me even more peace than what I already had. The kind of peace that for so long I had not known. Of all the answers I could have given to that doctor, I ended up saying: "Do you like my blanket?" I happily displayed it with a big smile on my face. It had been a long time since I shared a smile like that with anyone. For a second, it seemed as if I no longer had cancer. The pain I suffered was gone. This doctor was not your average doctor. When he smiled, I could see small flames of fire in his eyes that quickly disappeared, revealing that his eyes were blue—the type of blue you find in a crystalline pool.

He responded by smiling at me and saying: "I love your blanket." He put his hand on my chest and said: "That's why I love you so much because you have the heart of a child. This disease is not for death". He then turned around and left the room. I immediately started to fall asleep. The rest that eluded me since I had entered the hospital, I could finally find it that night.

In the morning, I woke up feeling new strength, but at the same time, I couldn't stop thinking about the doctor and the phone call with the youth group. I considered it might have been all a dream, from the young people calling to pray for me to the doctor who visited me. When I looked at my phone log, I was able to verify that the young people had called me. A little later, I confirmed with David that the call had dropped, and they could not get through again. But these young people finished the prayer and were determined to continue praying until the miracle occurred. David assured me that everything would be fine, as many people were praying for me.

The next day, in the evening, that doctor revisited me. Once again, a fragrant smell was released in the room. This time he approached my bed with a beautiful smile; touching my leg, he told me: "Rafael, it will be the last time you will see me, but I have come to tell you that this is not for death." I asked him for a hug, and he embraced me. I never wanted to let go. I felt the same peace that I found when I was in front of those golden stairs. The doctor left and did not visit me ever again. I never saw him again.

After a few days of not seeing that doctor again, I decided to ask my physician about Dr. Nazareth. I described him just as I saw him. With a worried face, he asked me what I was talking about. When he asked, "Who is Dr. Nazaret?" I answered: "The Doctor of all the doctors."

Chapter 11

I Don't Know How, But He Will Do It

Now, I knew for certain that my illness was not unto death. God had a mighty plan with all this. I didn't understand it, but I believed it. I was confident that in the end, everything would work out for the best. But before this happened, I had to deal with more evil than good. Without knowing it, I had just climbed aboard a roller coaster that seemingly would never end. One afternoon while my friend David was visiting me, the doctor came in to talk to me. This time he had more bad news to share. I could tell from the look he had in his eyes.

He looked at David and asked if he could allow us some privacy. Simply by saying this, I understood he did not have good news for me. Since David was one of my biggest supporters, I told him not to leave the room. I asked if he could please stay with me. Then the doctor faced my bed, struggling to find the words to start the conversation.

Both David and I were eager to hear his news. So, I said to the doctor: "You can't possibly have worse news for me than I have six months to live." Then the doctor looked at me and said: "Mr. Cuevas, after some examinations and meetings with my colleagues, we have come to the conclusion that there really is no possibility for you to survive this disease. But because you're young, we can see that the only way that you might have any chance of surviving is if we amputate your left leg. You may also soon end up losing your other leg in the process, as this cancer is very aggressive and is attempting to rush to the other bones.

I felt like a bucket of cold water was poured over me. David looked at the doctor and said, "You can't say that to him. There must be another way". David, filled with much Faith, looked at me and said: "Do not receive that news." The doctor recommended that I discuss it with my family and make a determination with them. I had to decide quickly since time was running out. But David charged me with Faith by telling me: "God is not going to allow your leg to be amputated." He laid his hands on me and declared once more that God would intervene. I spent a day in prayer while the doctors prepared everything to amputate my leg. If there is something that I am sure of, it is that while Faith does not deny reality, it can change it. In my prayer, I said to God: "If they cut off my leg and manage to stop this cancer, they will earn all the glory. I don't believe that losing my leg is part of the miracle that You have promised me. I don't see how losing my leg is part of this plan. But, let Your will be done, and not mine."

So I got my family together, and I talked to them about the doctor's recommendation. Everyone was alarmed by the news. They began asking questions and demanding a second opinion. However, we also began to pray. I could hear my mother's prayer as she said: "Lord, I dedicated him to you from my womb and asked you to make him an evangelist. Don't let my son's leg be amputated.

After everyone prayed, I spoke with the doctor and told him: "A few days ago, I had a vision where God told me that He had not finished with me in front of some golden stairs. If God still needs me, I'm going to require my legs for whatever He needs me to do. So even if I am lame, I will walk the rest of my days with my two legs as a sign that I fought with God and with men and won".

The doctor, in his confusion, only stared at me. I said, "Get your team ready and do what you have to do with this leg. If it is in the will of God, you cut it off. If not, God will intervene with His hand so that you do not do it. "Within days of declaring that word, the doctors were getting ready to perform the operation. My Faith did not deny the problem but was declaring that it would change the opinion of those doctors. What happened next impacted my life.

Mentally, I was preparing myself for what I thought would be the day of the operation. During that morning, the staff assured me that everything would go well and that I was in good hands. Later in the day, they came in search of me and were ready to take me to the operating room. All of a sudden, a big fight broke out in the hospital corridor. The shouting was very near to my room. I could hear the bickering voices of the people involved. That argument sounded as if it were occurring inside my room. Frantically, I asked my mother to please find out what was happening. My mother immediately left the room and returned just as quickly, with bewilderment on her face. She told me that she witnessed some doctors arguing. My doctor was among them. She supposed it had something to do with me, but my mother couldn't understand much English, and they all spoke English.

Minutes later, when the fight was no longer heard, a doctor, whom I had never seen, entered my room. She had tears in her eyes and tried to compose herself. She stood by my side to make the introduction, and after telling me her name, she began to explain: "I am a specialist in human conditions like the one you are experiencing today. I know you don't know me, but I am part of the team of doctors who are trying to help you. I was responsible for your biopsy, which confirmed you have cancer. I was also responsible for suggesting that your only hope was to amputate your leg. But this morning I had an experience with you. When I put your name on my computer, it led me to the YouTube channel. In a video, I watched you jump and run with a microphone in your hand. Apparently, you were preaching. I don't speak Spanish, nor do I understand it, but my office started shaking as if we were in the middle of an earthquake. I fell to my knees and felt the presence of God because even though I don't understand Spanish, I do understand God's language. He spoke to me and told me to save your leg because He will do a miracle with it and because you will preach His word again".

When something is not part of God's plan for your life, you can count on an intervention from God. The Bible says: "The steps of a good man are ordered by the Lord, and He delights in his way" (Psalm 37:23, NKJV). While it may seem otherwise, God is in control. You must trust in Him, no matter what you are experiencing. This doctor's declaration provoked peace in my life. I was encouraged and understood that this test dealt with more than a miracle; it involved a divine task for my life. It was then that God reminded me of where my calling began. I had become so focused on preaching at the crusades that I forgot my calling began by visiting the sick in the hospitals. Jesus said: "The healthy do not need a doctor, but the sick" (Matthew 9:12, ESV).

Jesus is revealing to us that He has not called us to entertain people. He also did not summon us to preach only to those people who look like us or speak like us. In other words, if you have the power to pray for the sick, why do you only use it on a platform when an audience is present? Why don't you bring the same power to hospitals where it's so needed? I managed to understand that God did not bring me to this hospital just to do a miracle in me, but He also allowed it so that I could impart the power that heals the sick to those who need it. That same power that saves and sets captives free. Realizing that it is not my legs that preach but my mouth, I got out of the bed and asked for a wheelchair. I encouraged myself by saying, "I refuse to be quiet. I'm going to preach even while God works a miracle.

Chapter 12

You'll Never Preach Again

In my humanity, I came to believe that I could no longer preach because, for many years, I only did it from platforms or altars. For me, preaching was about having a microphone in hand and an audience in front of you. How wrong I was! So God was about to use a voice to speak to me, to push me toward my assignment. I shared a room with another cancer patient; a single curtain divided us. He was a much older man than I. He couldn't speak; cancer didn't allow it. He looked worn out; there were signs of bitterness and sadness on his face.

One morning, I could hear his doctor talking to his wife in the hallway outside my door. I learned that the man was short on time, so they wanted to move him into a room where he could be alone with his family. His wife, devastated by the news, went somewhere else to cry where her husband could not watch her. Hours later, a voice spoke to me, but it was not God's voice that I heard.

This voice was not any good, nor did it impart peace into me. It spoke to me, saying, "You will never preach again."

As I heard it, I started to cry. Then it repeated those words: "You will never preach again." Hearing this voice for a second time created in me a sadness that consumed me. With a loud cry, I began to repeat what that evil voice was saying, "I am never going to preach again." Those who know me are fully aware that preaching is my greatest passion. It is the engine that drives me to live. Yet that voice made a grave mistake when it dared to speak to me for the third time: "You will not preach again." This time, instead of crying, I was charged with Faith. I came to and remembered that if there is one thing I am sure of, it is that the devil is a liar. Jesus himself describes him as the father of lies:

"You belong to your father the devil, and you want to carry out your father's wishes. He has been a murderer from the beginning, and he has not abided in the truth because there is no truth in him. When he speaks a lie, he speaks of his own; for he is a liar, and the
father of lies."
(John 8:44, NIV)

Therefore, whenever someone tells a lie, they are talking about something that has not happened and will never happen. It was then where I discovered that the truth is hiding in the contradiction of everything the devil tells us. If he tells you: "God is not going to perform this miracle," it is because he is sure that God will do it. In my case, he was trying to convince me that I would never preach again. Not only because he had imagined the completed miracle, but rather because he anticipated the day when I would write this book. His main goal was to steal my Faith. He could not foresee an opposite effect; instead of stealing my Faith, he increased it. I could hear the Voice of the Holy Spirit who revealed to me: "Nuni, the devil knows something about you that you don't know yet." In discovering the voice of the Spirit, I experienced supernatural strength. So much so that it seemed as if cancer no longer existed.

I began to move the curtain separating me from the cancer patient. I stared at him straight in the eyes and said with authority: "Hey, when you die, where are you going?" Due to the cancer, his vocal cords were no longer working, and he could not respond. He shrugged his shoulders, hinting that he did not know where he was going. I bowed my head and said, "Devil, if you hadn't spoken to me, you would have taken him away, but since you dared to speak to me, get ready, cause now I'm going to preach my best sermon; without a microphone and without a crowd." I shared the message of the Cross with this man and ended by letting him know that if he confessed Jesus with me, he would be saved. Then I asked him if he wanted to accept Jesus as his one and only Savior, and with tears in his eyes, he made a gesture with his head that assured me of a yes. Then I said, "Repeat with me: Lord Jesus, I accept you as my Savior." And the man opened his mouth and said, "Lord Jesus, I accept you as my Savior." A moment ago, this man could not speak, yet now he was confessing Jesus as Savior. God's presence filled that room.

As soon as he delivered the confession of Faith, accepting Jesus as his personal Savior, his wife entered the room. With joy and happiness, he said to his wife: "I'm leaving, I'm leaving!" With much surprise, she replied: "Are you talking?" The following words from that man were what impacted me the most. He said, "They came for me." She glanced at the door and said, "No one has come." I also looked but didn't see anyone coming. He asked her: "Can't you see those young people dressed in white, some even with flowers in their hands? They say they are going to take me to paradise". I raised my hands and began to praise God; in my praise, I said: "Devil, don't bother me because I'm going to preach."

Chapter 13

And He Gave Us Power

After this powerful experience, I understood that I could not let a disease stop me. I had to preach to as many people as I could. So at a specific time of day, I would get out of bed, get into the wheelchair and roam throughout the patient's rooms praying for them. I would first tell them about Jesus and then pray for them. One afternoon a pastor came to visit me. He found himself in my room, staring at an empty bed. When he asked the staff about me, no one could tell him where I was or what had happened to me. Worried, he was shouting my name through all the hospital corridors: "Nuni, Nuni, Nuni!" Finally, in his desperation, he encounters a nurse who did tell him where I was.

When he found me, I was praying for a cancer patient. Frantically, he entered the room in search of me. He grabbed my wheelchair and anxiously led me back to my room. "What are you doing outside your room?" he asked. "You're sick, and you have to rest. God forbid, you could end up catching another disease. And, what are you doing praying for cancer patients when you have cancer?" That is when I told him to stop my chair. I turned around to look at his face, and with authority and much respect, I told him: "Because Nuni has cancer, but Jesus does not."

Here's the kicker: If God doesn't do it for us, then we don't pray for Him to do it for others. God is God. So if he does not decide to perform the miracle, he continues to be God. On one occasion, John the Baptist sent messengers to find out if Jesus was the One sent by God or if they should keep looking. "And he sent them to Jesus, to ask Him: Are you the One who is to come, or will we wait for another?" (Luke 7:19, KJV). Some declare that John the Baptist was unsure whether Jesus, in truth, was the Son of God. I differ. John was convinced that Jesus was the Christ. He was present when a dove descended from heaven, and the audible voice of God was heard saying of Jesus: "This is my beloved Son, in whom I am well pleased" (Matthew 3:17, ESV). Of course, John knew that Jesus was the one sent from God. So why did he send messengers to ask Jesus that? I think it was to provoke a challenge since John also knew that Jesus had the power to get him out of jail. In Luke chapter 4, Jesus himself declared that he had also come to set the prisoners free. With this knowledge, when John the Baptist sends this message, he is clearly saying to Jesus: "If you are the Son of God, prove it to me by getting me out of jail." But Jesus replied: "Go, make known to John what you have seen and heard: the blind see, the lame walk, the lepers are cleansed, the deaf hear, the dead are raised, and the gospel is preached to the poor" (Luke 7:22, ESV).

In other words, Jesus was telling him, just because I don't get you out of jail, it doesn't mean I don't have the power to do it. Furthermore, it does not imply that I am not the One sent by God". In my case, because He hadn't healed me yet, it didn't mean He wasn't a healer. "Nuni has cancer, but Jesus does not have Cancer." Jesus will not stop working miracles because Nuni is not cured or because others are not healed when they ask for it. He is God, above all things. When He heals, He is God, and if He chooses not to, He is still God. Whenever you ask God for something, and He does not respond as you want, it does not mean that God has given up His identity. It also does not mean He has fallen short of His power to do it or that He has ceased to exist. The Bible records the words of God saying:

"For my thoughts are not your thoughts, neither are your ways my ways," said Jehovah. As the heavens are higher than the earth, so are my ways higher than your ways,

and my thoughts more than your thoughts."

(Isaiah 55: 8-9, ESV)

We must trust that God's plans are bigger and more powerful than our own. We shouldn't get frustrated when we ask God for a miracle, and He doesn't do it. In my case, I asked for a miracle, but God did not rush to deliver it to me because His plan went beyond healing me. God wanted to heal others first. If He had healed me when I first asked Him to, I would have left the hospital, never to return. But in God's perfect plan, although He wanted to heal me, He was initially going to use me to soothe all those who were suffering in front of me.

The Bible recounts the mighty miracles that Jesus performed on earth. Everywhere He went, miracles happened, just like the ones we mentioned earlier in Luke 7:22. On one occasion, Jesus gathered His disciples to transfer that same power. "Having gathered His twelve disciples, He gave them power and authority over all demons, and to heal diseases. And He sent them to preach the kingdom of God, and to heal the sick" (Luke 9: 1-2, ESV). So my question is, in today's world, why don't we see miracles like the ones Jesus did? The answer is simple. Because we have become accustomed to carrying this Word only to those who look and speak just like us, I call it entertainment. Or is a teacher dedicated to teaching the lesson to those who already know it? That would be a waste of time.

Medicine will not work on a healthy person. It can only be effective on those who require it. So how will we ever know the effectiveness of the power we carry if we do not give it to those who need it most? Instead, we immediately limit God by believing if He doesn't do it with me, He can't do it with others. What an erroneous way of thinking! We must learn that the power of God is unlimited. Let's pray until God does it and if the sick person is not healed, let's not stop there. Let's keep praying for the next sick person until we see God perform the miracle.

After my neighbor went to the Lord, I was sharing my room with another patient. This time, the patient was named Lucas, and he was a school teacher. He had a complicated illness that did not allow him to walk. So, his legs had swelled overnight. Lucas told me that he had been in the hospital for more than a month, and they still couldn't find the reason he couldn't walk or the source of his illness. I remember talking to Luke about Jesus and even mentioning that he carried the same name as one of Jesus' disciples.

Within days of being Lucas's new neighbor, I had an early-morning experience. While everyone was sleeping, and within all that silence, I opened my eyes to see something that I had never seen before. I was used to seeing many miracles, but this time the Spirit also revealed to me what caused diseases. I was able to see with my own eyes when a horrible beast came out of a room. It was a big monster with a huge tail that occupied the expansion of that corridor. It was full of ugly and dirty hair. The horns on the tip of its head followed in sequence to the other end of its massive tail. He wore a red torn cape on his back. His teeth were nasty, and drool was coming out of his mouth. A terrifying sound could be heard as he gnashed his teeth.

I confess to you that I was troubled when I saw it because I did not understand what it was or what it was doing there. As I watched him, I noticed how he dragged his leg while walking. Apparently, I was watching him from behind the wall of my room. That beast was wandering and gnashing his teeth, but he was totally unaware that I was watching him. So I asked God: "Who is that, and why is he here?" His answer left me speechless. God told me: "It is the principality that controls the diseases of this floor. He ensures that the people who come in here are not healed.

"And I said to God: "Why are you showing it to me?" "What does that have to do with me"? Then God answered me: "For this, I have brought you, and for this, I have prepared you. Since you were a child praying for the stuffed animals in your room, I have always been with you. In the same way, today, I will be with you again when you drive this beast off this floor. My Spirit is upon you." I realize that when you read this, you may feel confused and wonder what does a beast with diseases has to do with anything. Allow me to help you understand. The Bible says:

"Because we do not fight against blood and flesh, but against principalities, against powers, against the rulers of the darkness of this age, against spiritual hosts of wickedness in the heavenly regions."
(Ephesians 6:12, KJV)

There are battles that we cannot fight with medicine but can only take place in the Spirit. The Apostle Paul makes some statements in this 6th chapter of Ephesians, revealing to us that, in fact, there is a spiritual world of darkness. In that specific world, there are principalities, powers, and governors. This authoritative structure implies that they have dominion over different sectors of the spiritual world. "But for this, the Son of God appeared, to undo the works of the devil (1 John 3:8).

With this, I dare to say that evil spirits control 99% of the diseases in the world. The Bible says: "And there was a woman there who for eighteen years had a spirit of disease, and she was bent over and could not straighten up in any way" (Luke 13:11, ESV). It is made clear that the woman whom the book of Luke speaks of was ill, and she did not get better because there was an evil spirit that kept her that way. But in verse 12 of chapter 13 of Luke, we see Jesus tell her: "You are free." And when Jesus laid His hands on her, she was healed. In other words, when Jesus told her, "you are free," He was casting out the Spirit that this woman carried within her (Luke 13:12, ESV).

Now, here I was, looking at that principality that ruled that floor of the hospital. Since God revealed to me that He was with me, I got out of bed and took several steps towards the beast, but when I stopped and looked towards the bed, I could see that my body was still on the bed. It was there when I understood that I was entirely in the Spirit. As I previously stated, you cannot fight an evil spirit in the flesh. I rushed towards the beast. When he realized that I was in front of him, he tried to attack me but couldn't. Then I shouted: "Jehovah rebukes you!" I immediately spotted some white hands taking hold of mine, and together we grabbed the beast and suspended it in midair. Then I uttered the last cry: "Get out of this place in the name of Jesus!" As I declared those words, I witnessed the beast thrown down beyond the floor. It seemed as if the foundation of that hospital had opened, and that beast fell from floor to floor until finally, I could not see it again.

As soon as that beast disappears, I open my eyes to find myself in the hospital bed surrounded by doctors and nurses. According to them, the machines were beeping because I had lost my pulse. Sweaty and fatigued, I managed to take a breath. After several minutes, everyone asked me if I was okay. I replied, "Yes, I just fought a beast. But I cast him out in the Name of Jesus." You can imagine the expression on the faces of the doctors and nurses who cared for me when they heard me say such a statement.

Of all my nurses, there was one who was Christian; her name is Jaquelin. When everyone left the room, Jaquelin took my hands and prayed with me. Although the others did not understand what happened, Jaquelin understood it well. Several days after this experience, the patient Lucas was sent home. From one day to the next, his legs had healed, and he was already walking. So I was left alone in that room without anyone's company.

A few days after Lucas was released, I asked Jaquelin for the wheelchair to go out of the room. In my mind, I was going to visit more patients to pray for them. Jaquelin decided to keep me company. She took my chair and drove it down the hallway. As I passed the first room, I looked inside but saw that there was no one there. We went to the second room and when I looked there was no one there either. We went to the third, fourth, fifth, sixth, and there were no patients in the beds. I ordered Jaquelin to stop the chair and asked her, "How many patients are on this floor, including me?" She looked at me and said: "There is only one, and that is you" I said: "How is it possible that there is only one patient?" Her reply was as follows: "The doctors are also asking the same question as you. I can only tell you that the sick people on this floor were healed since you had that experience with the beast. Everyone is home, and you are the only one left."

Chapter 14

God Is In Control

Perhaps, after reading the previous chapter, you wonder, "If Nuni fought against this beast and all those who were sick are now well, then why was Nuni not healed with them?" The answer is the following: this beast controlled and influenced the diseases of this floor. I want to take this opportunity to clarify that not everyone who is sick is possessed by an evil spirit. Still, I want to be clear when I say that evil spirits influence 99% of all diseases. To own and to influence are two very different things.

Maybe you are asking yourself: if He is so good, why does God allow such bad things? To answer this in detail, I would need another book, but for now, I offer you this bible verse as a response: "And this is the condemnation: that light came into the world, and men loved darkness more than light, because their works were evil" (John 3:19, ESV). In other words, God is so good that He sent the light to the world, His Son, Jesus. But because of the bad decisions of men, including refusing to love Jesus, who came to give us life, we suffer from so many wicked things in this world. Human beings cannot pretend that even when they decide not to love God, they will continue to receive all the benefits of God.

Our Creator was clear when He said to Adam: "In the day that you eat of this fruit, you will surely die" (Genesis 2:17, ESV). People's actions have consequences. In this case, Adam's decision brought sickness and death to the world.

Now, if God is good, why was Nuni still sick? Why didn't God go ahead and heal him?

1. God was not done with my assignment

There were more people to whom I had to preach. Some who were waiting so that I would pray for them. And to calm my troubles, I was given a biblical verse that strengthened me in the moments of distress that were part of this phase of my illness.

"And we know that all things work together for good to those who love God, that is, those who are called according to his purpose."
(Romans 8:28, KJV)

In my illness, I trusted that what I was facing did not come to destroy me. I loved God and knew that all this, in the end, was going to work for my good. At the moment, I did not understand everything, but I knew that later on, I would comprehend.

2. God was proving to the devil the magnitude of my love for Him.

The Bible tells us about a man named Job, with whom I identify much. He was a man devoted to God. Job loved God very much and generously gave Him from everything he had. He served with great passion. Daily, Job raised an altar to God. This irritated the devil because he figured that Job was only faithful to God because of everything God did with him.

It came to pass that another day the sons of God came to present themselves before Jehovah, and Satan also came among them, presenting himself before Jehovah. And the Lord said to Satan, Where do you come from? Satan answered Jehovah, and said: To go about the earth, and to walk in it. And Jehovah said to Satan: Have you not considered my servant Job, that there is no other like him on earth, a perfect and upright man, fearing God and turning away from evil, and who still retains his integrity, even when you incited me against him to ruin him without cause? Responding Satan, he said to Jehovah: Skin for skin, all that a man has he will give for his life. But he now extends your hand, and he touches his bone and his flesh, and you will see if he does not blaspheme against you in your very presence. And the Lord said to Satan, Behold, he is in your hand; but he keeps his life. Then Satan left the presence of Jehovah, and struck Job with a malignant scabies from the sole of his foot to the crown of his head.

(Job 2: 1-7, ESV)

Let me make several points. The first point that I want to establish is that this is the second time Satan goes up to talk to God about Job. In other words, Satan had already discussed Job in chapter 1 but was unsuccessful in his first attempt. When Satan gets permission to execute the first attack on Job's house, he discovers that nothing he has done against Job could effectively prevent him from doing any of the things he usually did to please God. On the contrary, Job continues to love God and serve Him with great passion.

The second thing that I want to establish is Satan has no control over the lives of those that love and serve God. He cannot do anything against us, which God does not allow. For Satan to attack us, he must first ask God for permission. When God says no, he can't do anything to us.

The third thing I want to establish is that God himself asked Satan in verse 3: "Have you not considered my servant Job? There is no other like him on earth, a perfect and upright man, fearing God and turning away from evil, and that he still retains his integrity, even though you incited Me against him to ruin him without cause?" In other words, God was telling him: "Isn't it enough for you that you have already attacked him and Job still loves me? You want me to take everything from him, but I have no cause to do so because he is faithful to me." But Satan insists on making his point in verse 5. He still believed Job only loved God for all the blessings He had given him; health, prosperity, and a family. Here Satan asks God himself to touch Job: "But stretch out Your hand now, and touch his bone and his flesh, and he will surely curse You to Your face!"

Now I would like to answer the question raised at the beginning of this chapter. "If Nuni fought against this beast, and all those who were sick are now well, why wasn't Nuni healed?" I dare say that Satan failed to understand how, despite so much suffering, I could continue to preach and love God. My passion for God proved unshakable, even when my father fell on drugs. My devotion was tireless, although I faced hell every time I came home. The enemy could not fathom how I maintained my love for God, above all my problems. Even when I found myself rejected by the pastors and leaders of my city and felt despised by so many people, I always held God in high esteem. In the midst of the immense loneliness I felt during my travels, I loved God above it all. Not because of what He had given me, but because He is God. I don't need God to do me favors so that I could love Him. Just knowing that He created me and that He sent His Son to die on a cross, out of sheer love for me, is enough for me to love Him. Furthermore, the Bible says:

And I am convinced that nothing can ever separate us from the love of God. Neither death nor life, neither angels nor demons, neither our fears of today nor our worries of tomorrow. Not even the powers of hell can separate us from the love of God. No power in the heights or in the depths, in fact, nothing in all creation can ever separate us from the love of God, which is revealed in Christ Jesus our Lord.

(Romans 8: 38-39, NLT)

Since for Satan, it was not enough to bring all those attacks into my life, he said to God: "Why don't you touch the flesh and bones of Nuni with cancer? And then you will see how he will curse you." However, my reaction to God was: "If you heal me, we are friends, and if you do not heal me, we continue to be friends." I want you to know if God permits Satan to attack you, as he did with Job in verse 6, it is not because God wants to see you crying or because God wants to see you unhappy or depressed. When God allows the enemy to attack you, it is because he is saying to Satan: "Before you were an angelic being, but you did not know how to be faithful to me, but I am going to prove to you that this creation, formed from dust, will love me, and will adore me, despite this trial."

Finally, notice that in verse number 6, God tells him: "He is in your hand, but spare his life." I didn't have the problem, and neither do you. The problem is with Satan. He makes war on you, but he must protect you. He attacks you, yet, at the same time, he must make sure that you stay alive. And if God does not allow him to take your life in the midst of his attack, it is because He plans to give you the victory while you are still alive. Satan believes he knows everything. He thinks he knows how the movie of your life will end. He thought Job's worship would end the moment God made him sick. But here, from the lips of Job, a praise is born like never before. Unlike anything that has ever been heard in heaven or on earth.

And he said: "Naked I came from my mother's womb, and naked shall I return there. The Lord gave, and the Lord has taken away; Blessed be the name of the Lord."
(Job 1:21, NKJV)

"Shall we indeed accept good from God, and shall we not accept adversity?"
(Job 2:10, NKJV)

For I know that my Redeemer lives, and He shall stand at last on the earth.
(Job 19:25, NKJV)

So, I declare that beyond this attack, God is in control. A worship is about to come out of you like you have never seen or heard before. God is making it known to the devil that you can be what he never managed to be. Being a spirit, Satan failed in his faithfulness to God, but you, who are made of flesh, can be faithful to Him. He also wants the enemy to know that you do not love God for what He can give you, but because He is God. The Lord has not allowed this disease because you have failed Him; on the contrary, you are one of the greatest warriors He has in His Kingdom. And that's why He's chosen you. Because only you can handle a trial like the one you are going through or the one I was facing.

After all this is said and done, get ready, because just as God did with Job, He will also do with you. Giving you back a double portion of everything the devil stole from you. The upcoming weight of Glory will be heavier in your life. This trial has an expiration date. Just as it came, it has to go! The Bible says:

"For our present troubles are small and won't last very long. Yet they produce for us a glory that vastly outweighs them and will last forever!"

(2 Corinthians 4:17, NLT)

What I used to call a death threat, like cancer is, God calls a mild test. In other words, this test cannot beat my God. He is invincible! No one has ever been able to conquer Him. Neither cancer nor any disease in this world can go head-to-head with my God. The second fact that this verse establishes is that the trial before you is momentary; it will not last forever. And finally, this test is not taking away from you; on the contrary, it produces within you more Glory every day. It is creating in you more presence of God. Instead of separating you from God, it is drawing you closer to Him. You are developing skills in you that you did not have before. The enemy will regret having asked God to send you such a test.

Celebrate because this fight is coming to an end. Celebrate because you will come out stronger than you were.

Chapter 15

By His Stripes, We Are Healed

After three months in that hospital, I was transferred to the University Hospital in Newark, NJ, where a group of oncologists and orthopedics would treat my case. I was referred to them by the same doctor who saved my leg. I remember when they brought me into the ambulance that would transport me to the new hospital. Because of my illness, I had been feeling like a prisoner. From the moment I was taken to the hospital and diagnosed until the transfer, I had not been outside. They never allowed me an opportunity to return home.

The University Hospital was across from my home. When we drove by the house, the pain and sadness deepened. I cried when I saw my house through the window of that ambulance because I wanted to go back to what I used to identify as a hell of a home. I would rather deal with an addicted father and parents in a dysfunctional marriage than with a disease like cancer. I was a hospital prisoner simply for loving God. But even still, I said to God:

"Let Your will be done and not mine."

Upon arriving at my new home, I had to meet my new oncologist. Now pay close attention to what I am about to tell you. The initial doctor who diagnosed my cancer, the same one who told me: "You have six months to live", died six months later. When he told me that I would not survive, I replied: "By His stripes, we are healed" (see Isaiah 53: 5). He then looked at me and said, "I don't believe in that." For lack of faith, when cancer knocked on his door, he died. The answer to his cancer was found in simply believing in the power of Jesus' wounds. My question is, how hard is it to believe? Believing costs nothing..

Now, my new doctor looks at me and says, "Rafael, we'll make you as comfortable as possible in the time you stay here." I replied, "Don't worry, I don't have much time here. Not because I will die, but because I will be healed. By His stripes, we are healed." With a smile, she glanced at me. Then she looked at my mother and said, "I don't understand, but it's okay." I continued saying: "Let's talk doctor to doctor." With a beautiful smile, the doctor accepted: "Let's talk." So I stated: "As a doctor, you know that there are 39 strands of the diseases worldwide. Jesus received 39 lashes on His back. Each lash left a wound.

One of those wounds is called cancer." In amazement, she said: "Amen."

Long before Jesus came to earth, the prophet Isaiah had a vision. In his vision, he witnessed the Lamb of God (Jesus) and how he was scourged and beaten for our sins and diseases.

"But He was wounded for our transgressions; He was bruised for our iniquities. The chastisement for our peace was upon Him, and by His stripes, we are healed."
(Isaiah 53:5, NKJV)

Keep in mind that when Isaiah spoke about this, it was hundreds of years before the birth of Jesus. In other words, this was not a last-minute improvisation by God. He always has a plan. Long before illness could come, God had already prepared the miracle. Human beings tend to wait until after a disease arrives to create an antidote, but this antidote was already available in God long before cancer existed.

You must understand, Jesus came to repair what Adam ruined in the Garden of Eden. By eating from the forbidden tree, Adam and Eve brought sin into the world.

Immediately, sin corrupts everything: nature, animals, and man, causing death and disease. So, by dying on the Cross, Jesus had to crucify not only sin but also all that sin provided; things like death and disease. Therefore, when God shows Isaiah this vision of Jesus, the prophet mentions not only sin (the cause) but also disease (the effect). The most striking thing about this verse is that, in the original text, Isaiah does not actually say, "By His wounds." Instead, He says, "By His wound." In other words, there were 39 stripes, but only one is enough to heal you. A single stripe is enough to forgive you. A single stripe is enough to save you. One is enough to set you free.

Some people will never read the Bible. This was the case with this doctor, who had never even picked up a Bible. But I've got good news for you. Every time a believer walks down the street, the world is given an opportunity to read the Bible. So this doctor was on the verge of reading her first chapter of the Bible. Not through sheets of paper, but rather through the demonstration of my deeds. Since the Bible is not meant to be known, it is intended to be lived.

Chapter 16

I Am Death

After meeting the new team of doctors, and because the cancer was in an advanced stage, consuming all the bones in my left leg, they decided to give me chemotherapy. The strongest kind they could give me. In reality, I had no idea what I was going to face. I vividly remember when they put this dark orange bag next to my IV fluids and covered it with another black bag. When I saw this, I said to myself: "This is easy. Is this chemotherapy? Only that chemotherapy lasted five days at a time, which meant that once the liquid fully entered my body, they immediately put in a new bag. The treatment process repeated continuously from Monday until Friday, finally giving me a week-long break. As soon as the week of rest was over, they immediately brought back that dark and orange bag with the black plastic cover.

Trust me, that bag turned into a torture device for me. Every day I felt as if it was telling me I was dying. That in truth, its job was not to heal me; it was to torture me until the day when cancer finally managed to take my life. I heard it say, "I will slowly take all your health away, little by little, starting with your hair." With every loss, it announced that death was closer to me. While the doctors saw a bag full of hope, I only knew a bag of torture. A reminder that reality had numbered my days. That bag caused me nausea, vomiting, dizziness, fever, and chills. I even felt it when the serum made its way through the pores of my body. The smell of perspiration emanating from my pores was like sulfur. All around me, it stank like hell.

Every twenty minutes, the symptoms mentioned above would transpire. I felt like that bag was going to drive me crazy. It was like a roller coaster that never wanted to end. I went through the chills, vomiting, dizziness, and fevers. I would start sweating as if I were in a sauna. If I were to describe what chemotherapy is, I would tell you it is a virus integrated into your body — one that enters to fight another virus called cancer and turns the whole body into the battlefield. In this war, the innocent are paying the consequences. Here, the innocent party would be described as my skin, my hair, my eyes, and all my senses. It's like having the flu 24 hours a day, 7 days a week.

I confess that even while writing this chapter, for a moment, as I re-lived the memory of what happened, I felt like I was losing my breath. Simply by closing my eyes for a second, I can picture myself in that depressing room, remembering the beginning of my torture. Every time another drop fell, not only did the little health I had left disappeared, but also those people who claimed to be my friends. Many stopped visiting me; even the ministers were evident in their absence. I even stopped hearing God's voice. As I share these memories, my heart cannot help but feel a considerable amount of pain. But I can still rejoice because if I can feel that pain, it means I am still alive. The dead cannot feel or suffer.

They placed a port inside the right side of my chest, which facilitated an entryway to one of the central veins of my body. Through that port, I would receive the chemotherapy fluids, and thus it would quickly spread throughout my body, attacking every cancerous cell. On the first day when they attached the bag, I instantly felt the first few drops of chemotherapy as they entered my veins. My body felt strange. I understood that my fight was only beginning. I still cannot say which is worse; cancer or chemotherapy. All I can tell you is that I do not wish any of this, even on my worst enemy. When the first Friday of the treatment arrived, during the early hours, I received a visitor. And no, it wasn't the type of visitor I wished to have.

During my battle with cancer, I can count on the

fingers of my left hand how many pastors and evangelists came to visit me. When I most wanted their company, hoping to receive prayer and a declaration of life, I would then learn they were part of those expecting the day when my mother would break the news of my death due to my cancer. I wondered, where was the Faith that they claimed to have. Or maybe they did have some but weren't willing to use it for my healing. The good thing about all of this is that God does not need the Faith of others to heal you or lift you up. Your own Faith is more than enough to move God in your favor. I quickly discovered, not everyone who carries a title bears the anointing that the title brings. As a result, I will tell you to always place your trust in God, not in men. They will fail you, but God will never fail you. The Bible says:

"Looking unto Jesus, the author and finisher of our faith, who for the joy that was set before Him endured the cross, despising the shame, and has sat down at the right hand of the throne of God."
(Hebrews 12:2, RVR1960)

If you keep your eyes on men, you will find yourself disappointed, as it is human nature to fail. But the nature of God is to be faithful to you. Having said this, if my miracle had depended on those ministers, I would have died.

So, in the early morning, on the first Friday of chemotherapy, I received a horrible visitor. As I heard the footsteps approaching my room, I could identify them as someone with boots. From the sound, it seemed like they were cowboy boots. The fear I felt as he strolled towards me assured me that what was nearing my room was unpleasant. I knew his intentions were up to no good because God does not cause fear but peace and courage.

"For God has not given us a spirit of fear, but of power
and of love and of a sound mind."
(2 Timothy 1:7, NKJV)

When I opened my eyes I saw a man whose height reached to the ceiling. He had the same black hat that I had seen in my childhood, and a black jacket that reached down to his feet. Yes, it was the same man who visited my father when I was a kid. I did not understand why he was in my room. He told me: "I am death." Immediately, I saw in front of me a coffin.

That character, claiming to be death, opened the coffin and while he was opening it said to me: "This is what

I'm going to do with you." He took my body and placed me inside. When I tried to fight him and get out of that coffin, I couldn't, because my body was paralyzed. I couldn't open my mouth either, I could only hear the voice of my thoughts.

Motionless, I watched death standing behind my head, which rested on the pillow of that coffin. Then I noticed the tool he had in his hand was the same one used by funeral homes to accommodate the dead inside the coffin, prior to closing the box. While he was placing that instrument, he told me: "This is what I am going to do with you and with your calling." Then I started to feel my body sinking into the coffin. As he slowly closed the coffin, I had no choice but to watch as the darkness enveloped me. When he finally closed it completely, I began to notice the coffin descending into the ground. At this point, I could no longer see the man, but I could hear him. While throwing dirt on the coffin, he repeated to me again: "This is what I'm going to do with you." At that moment, I began to cry out to God in my mind.

The madness of all this was that while I was going through this experience, my dad was living the same episode at my house. My father recounts how he encountered the same character that I just described. He was before him saying: "This is what I'm going to do with your son." When my dad looked, he could see my body inside the coffin, the flowers and the people crying in a church, while everyone sang the hymn "Hallelujah". In my father's description, he watched as that character stood next to my head and closed the coffin. He heard this evil man repeating once again: "This is what I'm going to do with your son." Meanwhile, I'm living the same incident as my dad, only I was inside the coffin, and he was outside.

When I realized that he was burying me, I said to God in my mind: "I am yours. I always have been and always will be. Jesus, death does not have more authority than You." When I said those words, my mouth was free to speak, and I screamed: "Death, I am not yours! I belong to Jesus! He defeated you on the Cross of Calvary. And only He has the keys of death. I'm not going to die. God told me that He still has much work for me. As I declared those words, the coffin opened. Suddenly, I began to flee with great desperation. So much so that without realizing it, I was getting out of bed. I only saw a coffin. I could not see a hospital bed. My father was holding me down because I was falling off the bed. But still, I couldn't see my dad; I only saw an open coffin in front of me. I was trying to get out as quickly as possible, yet my father hugged me and said, "You are not going to die. You belong to Christ; you belong to Christ. Daddy is here. You belong to Christ." At last, my natural eyes were opened, and I could finally see my father. I told him: "Death visited me." His response was: "I know, that's why I'm here. You belong to Christ."

A few days later, they sat me down for a bath. I couldn't handle the smell coming out of my pores. While I was bathing, I began to wash my hair. My faith was so great that I believed my hair would never fall out. But while I was rinsing it off, I noticed much hair all over my hands and the bathtub floor. I felt an extreme burning sensation on my scalp. When I saw that the water washed away all my hair, I went crazy screaming. My father walked up to me, and when he saw me without hair, he cried and said, "Samson also lost his hair, but God gave it back to him." Those who witnessed my hairless head would say, you are a man, and bald men look good. They didn't understand that, while they looked at a boy without hair, I saw a boy surrounded by death. This struggle was more intense than I had previously imagined since it was not only against cancer but against death itself.

Chapter 17

Oh Death, I Will Be Your Death

Now it was clear that my fight was not only against cancer but also against death itself. People struggle with different types of cancer and at different stages. Depending on the stage of cancer, the likelihood of the person being cured is known. But when you fight in the fourth stage, you are no longer just fighting the disease. You are going against death hand to hand, face to face. Clearly, no one wants to die. We all long for a prolonged life. In my case, I was only 22 years old. I had so much ahead of me. If truth be told, I was not afraid of the actual death. I was confident that for those who are in Christ, there is a paradise awaiting.

Jesus said:

"If anyone serves Me, let him follow Me; and where I am, there My servant will be also. If anyone serves Me, my Father will honor him."
(John 12:26, NKJV)

"In My Father's house are many mansions; if it were not so, I would have told you. I go to prepare a place for you."
(John 14:2, NKJV)

Therefore, for those who die in Christ, there should be no worries. Heaven itself awaits us. It is for this exact reason that death was so angry with me. For it knew that if I died, I won, and if I lived, I won.

"For to me, to live is Christ, and to die is gain."
(Philippians 1:21, NKJV)

The only way death can defeat us is when we are outside of Christ, because there, we find the manifestation of the second death. Allow me to explain: In the Garden of Eden, God was clear in His instructions to Adam and Eve when He told them: "Of every tree, you can eat less of the tree of the knowledge of good and evil. For in the day you eat from it, you will surely die" (Genesis 2:17, NIV). However, when Eve eats the forbidden fruit, she did not immediately fall dead to the ground. When Adam sees that nothing happened to Eve, he too decided to eat. But the death that God was speaking of implicated beyond the physical state; it included the condition of the soul. The human soul is the very breath of God, which was "breathed so that man might be a living creature" (see Genesis 2:7). The soul is what is truly responsible for keeping the body alive. Not only does it sustain the physical frame, but it also manages it. In other words, the body is just a vehicle that allows the soul to operate on earth. When the body dies, the soul leaves the corpse and goes to a place of eternity. When departing, it is supposed to return to God since it came from Him. But the final destination depends on how the person lived on earth. It is based primarily on whether the person accepted Jesus as his Savior since He is the only way to salvation and the gateway to heaven. Therefore, the soul can return to dwell with God, but only through Jesus.

"I am the door; whoever enters through me will be saved; and he will come in and go out and find pasture." (John 10: 9, ESV)

Many get angry when questioning if God is so good, why does He allow people to go to hell? My response to them is this: God is so good that he respects the decisions a person makes on earth. When someone determines he wants nothing to do with Jesus, God takes his preference into account at the time of death. Recognizing that they chose to live apart from Jesus in their years of life, it is also understood that in eternity they will not want to have anything to do with Him either. So God sends them to the only place where He does not dwell.

Adam and Eve unlatched the door to hell. And this is the second death. A death of perdition. A damning death. The one that for centuries has led the disobedient into captivity. Jesus spoke about this place while telling the disciples about a king who died and arrived at a place of extreme heat and torture (see Luke 16: 19-31). The king asked permission to go out and notify his brothers about the existence of that place. God answered the king by reminding him that He had sent prophets to earth for that reason, so that they could announce it to the world.

Since humanity managed to open the gates of hell, to have a chance at redemption, men found themselves before the priests offering a sacrifice for the forgiveness of their sins. The richest brought him a lamb, and the poorest a dove. On their behalf, the priest would bring these sacrifices to the altar so that God would forgive their sins and deliver them from the second death (see Leviticus 12: 6). Now, this is an unavoidable fact: Every man who is born must face death. Even Jesus himself was born to confront and overcome death. For this reason, many threats came to Him, even from the womb of His mother.

Through the visitation of the Holy Spirit, Jesus was conceived in the womb of Mary. But that was an inconceivable concept before carnal men who would never accept that Mary became pregnant by the work of the Holy Spirit (see Matthew 1:18). Logic dictates clearly that only through a man can a woman conceive. But God is not limited by logic. This ability is precisely what makes God, God! Hence, revealing Him as the God of the impossible.

The first threat existed within the law, which demanded that anyone found guilty of fornication or adultery must be stoned to death for their sin, along with the accomplice. Upon hearing of her pregnancy, Joseph, Mary's betrothed, attempted to flee since he had not touched her yet. His logic told him that Mary had been with another man, but the angel of Jehovah visited him, confirming that everything was the work of the Holy Spirit. As previously discussed in the first chapter of this book, the second attempt occurred when Jesus was born and King

Herod sought to kill Him (see Matthew 1:20). Jesus needed to face death as a man since no one could ever defeat something unless they're willing to confront it.

Let us not forget that Jesus was challenging both; physical death and also that of the soul. In Matthew 4, we find Him alone in the desert facing Satan. Notice how every temptation presented by Satan intended to provoke Jesus into losing his life and soul. However, the Bible declares that He was perfect in everything.

"Christ never sinned; He never told a lie. He never answered back when insulted; when He suffered, He did not threaten to get even. He left his case in the hands of God, who always judges fairly"
(1 Peter 2:22-23, TLB)

If Jesus had sinned, He would have ruined the perfect plan of becoming the Lamb of God which came down from heaven to forgive the sin of all humanity.

"The next day John saw Jesus coming toward him, and said, 'Behold! The Lamb of God who takes away the sin of the world!'"

(John 1:29 NKJV)

Having established this point, one can better appreciate why the perfection of Jesus and His ability to reach the Cross was a significant inconvenience for death. Death was determined to keep Jesus as far away from the Cross as possible, for it was a place of sacrifice. If Jesus managed to be sinless when coming in contact with the Cross, He would guarantee death's demise. Therefore, as Jesus took our sins upon His back, He was gaining access to crucifixion. In an instant, death started celebrating, for only a sinner could die on a cross. For a moment, it seemed as if Jesus had been defeated. Death appeared to have won. In the enemy's viewpoint, the continued captivity of humanity was at hand because no one could save them. As he looked towards the Cross, death could only see the sin that Jesus had laid on himself, for He crucified our sins together with Him.

For this reason, when He died, Jesus could not immediately enter paradise, for He carried humanity's sin.

Before the Cross took place, every time, Jesus freed someone and said: "Your sins are forgiven," with those same words, He took responsibility for that person's sin. As He brought deliverance to individuals, He gradually took the place of each sinner, until finally, on the Cross of Calvary, at once, the sins of the whole world were cast upon Him as He said: "Father, forgive them, for they don't know what they do" (Luke 23:34, NIV).

As the life of Jesus faded away, death was celebrating, mainly because it knew that the consequence, the penalty of all that sin upon His shoulders, earned Jesus a place in hell. At last, the forces of evil managed to gain access to Him. There was no avoiding it. Because He carried our sins, Jesus had to face the dark prisons of hell. Yet death could not anticipate how this complicated matters for hell. For even though Jesus bore the sins of the world, in Him there was none to be found. His sinless status meant death had no power over Him. It could not keep Him nor make Him its prisoner.

At this juncture, the never before seen happened. Jesus took control of hell and began preaching the gospel to all those imprisoned there. As the God of justice, who came down to earth offering a second chance to all mankind, He took the time to provide that same opportunity for those who died long before Jesus was born. Just like He preached to the living, He now preached to the dead. Suddenly, what appeared to be defeat in the face of death was now exposed as God's perfect plan to overcome death, once and for all. My sin upon Him was the key that allowed Him to enter, but His perfection was the key that allowed the exit (see 1 Peter 3:18,19). Considering the words of King David, I dare say that he prophetically foretold that Jesus would visit hell to defeat this second death and preach to those captives.

"If I ascend to heaven, you are there: and if I make my footstool in hell, behold, You are there"
(Psalm 139:8, ESV)

I would have liked to see the face of death, as it realized Jesus had come to be their prisoner, but to bring freedom to the captives and take them with Him to heaven. Yes! He took them with Him to paradise. For preaching is not preaching if there is no call for repentance.

"For this reason, he says: Going up on high,
He led captivity captive, and gave gifts to men."
(Ephesians 4: 8, NIV)

Clearly, the Word of God establishes; Jesus not only freed those who heard His message but also empowered all who believe in Him so that death no longer has power over us. At our time of death, we no longer have to enter a dark prison. Christ paid the price of our freedom.

Around the same time of the crucifixion, there were certain people who died and whose families had mourned and buried them. The death of Jesus proved so powerful that, while Jesus perished on the Cross, they began to rise again (Matthew 27:52). What strikes me most about this is that Jesus started to deliver deadly blows to death within an instant of His death. Upon arriving and freeing the captives, Jesus became death's death. Now, consider the following: if Jesus could raise the dead during His death, what would he not do to death now that He is alive and sitting at the right hand of His Father God (Mark 16:19). It is no wonder the devil and his demons fear the Name of Jesus mentioned on the earth. Well, every time you proclaim "JESUS," you remind the devil of the beating He gave him on earth. Not as God, but as a man. So if Jesus could defeat death as a man, how much more could He now do to death as my God? For this reason, death is so afraid of a believer. Especially since the same Jesus, who now lives seated on His throne at the Father's right hand, also lives in us, giving us access to that same power.

Therefore, I dedicate this chapter to death. To remind you that you are defeated. Many claimed to be the way of salvation but have since died, like Buddha, Muhammad, Gandhi. But when Jesus died, He rose again on the third day. He never died again, but he ascended to heaven in life. In the Book of Revelation, God manifested Himself to the Apostle John, who then said:

"When I saw Him, I fell as dead at His feet.
And He put His right hand on me, saying to me: Do not be afraid; I am the first, and the last; and the one who lives, and was dead; but behold, I live forever and ever, amen.
And I have the keys of death and Hades."
(Revelation 1: 17-19)

Jesus will never die. He is alive forever. So there is no need to fear death. Death must be afraid of Him, for

Jesus is death's death. Somehow, it managed to forget the warning God gave many years before Jesus came to die when He said:

"From the hand of Sheol I will redeem them,
I will deliver them from death. Oh death,
I will be your death; and I will be your destruction, oh
Sheol; compassion will be hidden from my sight."
(Hosea 13:14, ESV)

Having said all this, if you are in Jesus, don't be afraid of death. Instead, be afraid to die without first reaching your full potential. Be afraid of dying, with all those dreams still inside you. Be afraid of dying before having realized all your objectives. Be afraid of dying with all those books still inside you, just as this book was inside me. At all costs, you have to avoid dying full. Die empty. Leave all the divine deposits you have ever received here on earth. Cede nothing to death. You can start by emptying yourself here on earth. Don't take anything with you.

I did not fear death. My fear was dying while this book was still in me, having never been published. Dying full of sermons that I was meant to preach. There was still a lot left in my tank. Someday I would become a husband, a father, a grandfather. There was much to be done. So today, you too can renounce death. Put an end to death in your life. Tell it that you belong to Jesus. That you still have glorious achievements ahead of you. That God is not finished with you. The day He is finally done with you, death will not be the one who will come in search of you; it will be Jesus himself.

God is not the God of the dead, but of the living. With this, I assure you that God does not kill anyone; He only moves them from one place to another. Make sure that when your moment to be moved arrives, you are drawn even closer to God and not far away from Him.

Chapter 18

I Once Was Blind, But Now I See

In previous chapters, I mentioned that this fight with cancer would make me live what I had preached for years, since the sermons that most impact the world are not those you preach through a microphone, but those you live when the microphone is not in your hand. The intensity of the chemotherapy got worse and worse. So much so that the pain in my bones increased to the point it burned my skin. I no longer had any hair left. My eyes turned yellow. My skin had changed color, my natural skin color took flight, and now my complexion was a purplish tone. I weighed almost 180 pounds since every meal I ate left my mouth as soon as it entered. To top it all off, the inside of my mouth was full of sores, and I had lost the taste of food.

I could barely speak. I had lost my smile, and when I tried to find it, it seemed to me as if it had disappeared forever. That boy, who was often laughing out loud, was now known for his silence. The contagious laugh, which inspired a smile in others, turned into a constant cry. You may wonder, but why bother crying if God told you that He would heal you? But there were long days when it seemed as if my reality was winning over faith. Days when I felt as if God was taking too long with my miracle. So much so that I became convinced God had forgotten me. If you have ever thought the same thing, don't feel bad. At some point or another, we all felt this way, especially when we didn't see the miracle happen as soon as we wanted. As if God could ever forget us. Job himself expressed how he felt forgotten when he inquired of God: "Why do you hide Your face and consider me Your enemy?" (Job 13:24). Job's question brings us to the understanding that he had been praying to God, but God would not respond to him. That was precisely how I found myself—praying and praying without hearing anything from God. So, what do we do when we pray, and God does not answer us? Well, we keep on praying. We keep believing. We must not stop. We stand firm upon faith, waiting until God does something.

Job even assumed God was angry with him, but from his experience, I learned two things: (1) That there is nothing wrong with crying. (2) That if you are going to cry, you have to cry with Faith. Your tears will become the water that God will use to make your miracle flourish. The psalmist declares that those who sow with tears will reap with shouts of joy.

"He who walks with tears,
bearing the seed of the sowing, will indeed return
with shouts of joy, bringing his sheaves."
(Psalm 126: 5-6, ESV)

Tears tend to conceal the revelation. When Jesus wept before Lazarus' tomb, the people said, "He weeps because He loved him" (John 11:36-37). However, I beg to differ. Jesus was not crying due to the death of Lazarus, but because among these people existed a lack of Faith. Mary, Lazarus' sister, told Him: "If you had been here, my brother would not have died." She had enough Faith to believe that Jesus could heal the sick but not raise the dead. Martha also said to Him: "If You had been here, my brother would not have died." Her Faith was equal to the dwellers of that village. They all agreed; Jesus had the power to heal the sick, just not to raise the dead.

God allowed the death of Lazarus so that everyone in that town would know that Jesus not only heals the sick, but He also raises the dead. As He cried, within His tears, Jesus reveals to us that even when the whole village suffers from a lack of Faith, God can work miracles. Jesus then said: "Father, I thank you for having heard me. I am not saying this because of You, but for the sake of those around me". In other words, while Jesus cried because of the insufficiency of Faith among the people, despite His tears, God showed Him that if He only pronounced the name of Lazarus, His dead friend would come out alive from that tomb. That miracle was never going to happen through the Faith of those people; rather, it only happened through the Faith of Jesus. After what happened on that occasion, today, I dare to say that if you do not have much Faith in your miracle, count on Jesus, He always has enough for you.

After He cried, Jesus said: "Roll the stone" (John 11:39). So I'll tell you: get ready! If you have cried and cried a lot, prepare for it because your salvation is near. For Jesus not only heals the sick, but He also raises the dead. Whatever difficulty you may face has not come to destroy you; it is here to show you that Jesus also raises the dead. In other words, Jesus is capable of all things. Don't limit Him!

In my case, before God could heal me from cancer, He would show me that he not only had the power to cure me of cancer, but also the power to heal my eyesight. One afternoon, during weeks of intensive chemotherapy, I noticed my vision blurring as I spoke to my mother. As a reaction, I repeatedly began to open and close my eyes. I started to rub my eyes with my hands. My first thought was it could have resulted from inadequate rest, as I found it difficult to sleep. Yet cancer, along with intensive chemotherapy, worked together to steal my sight. Right then and there, when my eyesight began to fade, there was nothing I could do to stop it, so I began to freak out. When I finally realized that everything went blank until I was in complete darkness, I screamed and sobbed in despair. I felt this was not normal, my sight was stolen, and it would never be returned to me.

When I said to her: "Mom, I can't see you. I lost my sight. Get help!" my mother immediately ran out searching for the nurse. I couldn't see anything, absolutely nothing. I was worried and afraid of losing my ability to see because not only had I stopped walking, but now, to top it off, I was completely blind. My doctor told my mother that the cancer was progressing and that I would never recover my sight. This happened on a Wednesday afternoon. Later, I discovered that we should never focus on the things we have lost. Instead, we should always rejoice in what remains. God will not make a miracle out of the things you have lost. He will use whatever you have left to do wonders. And if by chance you are among those who say: "I have nothing left," the Bible teaches us, "God multiplies strength where there are none" (Isaiah 49:29). This scripture means that, even if you are among those who say the enemy has stolen everything from you, whenever God is ready to perform a miracle on your behalf, nothing will depend on your substance.

I had lost my hair, walking ability, weight, and now my eyesight, but I had yet to lose Faith. If there is something I am sure of, it is that the enemy can steal many things from us, but he cannot rob us of our Faith. "Now faith is the substance of things hoped for, the evidence of things not seen" (Hebrews 11:1, NKJV). For we do not walk by sight, but by Faith. It is a fact that my legs could no longer walk, and my eyes refused to see; even so, although blind and disabled, my Faith had the strength to help me reach my miracle. And where was my miracle? In the presence of God. Therefore, I began to pray intensely. Wednesday and Thursday had passed, and it was already Friday. The sun was rising, and the nursing morning shift started. I could tell, because although I was unable to see a clock or watch the sunrise, I could hear the nurses in the hallway greeting each other: "Good morning." This exchange made me aware of the time at 6 a.m. when the night shift was over.

The Bible says: "Weeping may endure for the night, but joy comes in the morning" (Psalm 30: 5). This scripture encourages us to believe that the test will not come to stay with you forever. I was tired of crying, and now I was ready to snatch my miracle. I firmly believe that the Bible is not meant to be known; it is intended to be lived. It is full of inspiration and Faith to help us overcome our crisis. From all the wonders that Jesus performed, the Book of Mark recounts one of the miracles that fascinates me most (Mark 10:46). It's about a blind man shouting: "Son of David, have mercy on me," but the surrounding people told him to be quiet. In most cases, the closer you are to your miracle, the more resistance you find. If you have any fight left, don't give up. You are closer to your miracle than ever. Historians say that in the old days, when someone was blind, they were not allowed to be on the same path as the healthy. Back then, there was a common belief that blindness was a curse. They lived under the misconception that either the person or their ancestors must have done something wrong to provoke God's wrath and punishment through blindness.

I can identify a lot with this. Especially when the things that many leaders in my city were saying about me reached my ears; I must have done something wrong in order for God to give me cancer. That is what religion does; it believes that every bad thing that happens in life is a consequential punishment. Nevertheless, this attitude is contrary to what Jesus said on another occasion when He was about to heal another sick person: "This happened so that God could be glorified" (John 9:3). Whenever Bartimaeus started screaming, the crowd immediately ordered him to remain silent. He was reprimanded for his shouting. The law clearly stipulated that if you were blind, your place was begging by the roadside, and the only time you should be heard shouting is when someone gave you an offering. Only then could you, with a loud voice, shout the name of the person who showed you charity. But here, we see a blind man crying out the name of Jesus, someone who had yet to offer him money and much less healing.

Here, I discovered the secret of miracles. Whenever you celebrate Jesus as Bartimaeus did, God's grace is manifested in your life long before His miracle. Hence, on this occasion, the Hebrew word celebrate is defined as a feast that occurs long before the victory. Celebrating, at that time, would be a glorious party after a great victory. Faith leads you to celebrate before it is done. So now, not only was I going to believe, I was going to celebrate Jesus long before He healed me. There are moments in times when we have to scream. We cannot keep silent. If Bartimaeus had kept quiet, Jesus would have passed by and would never have healed him, but by shouting, he captured Jesus' attention.

Bartimaeus was one of the stories that I had preached the most in my childhood. Although I was preaching about a blind man who shouted "Jesus," in reality, I did not have the slightest idea of what it was like to be a blind man. Now that I knew what it was like to be blind, as soon as I heard the nurses say, "Good morning," I began to shout, "Son of David, have mercy on me." With a loud voice, I entered into intense adoration. "Son of David, have mercy on me. Son of David, have mercy on me." When a nurse came in to shut me up, I knew I was very close to a miracle. "Mr. Cuevas, have you gone crazy? Shut up! The patients are terrified." Precisely when she was telling me to: "shut up, the African nurse who prayed with me every morning was entering the room. That nurse, filled with the Holy Spirit, told her: "You shut up and get out of the room! Let him scream! As he screams, God returns his sight". She approached me and said: "Shout Rafael, and don't stop! Shout, let the heavens hear you!" At that moment, I gave one more cry.

With tears in my eyes, I felt something supernatural entering that hospital room. I began to notice that the black landscape became white, and the white became blurred colors. Then the blurred colors started to lighten until finally, I could see again. When my doctor visited me that afternoon, her greeting was: "They say you were screaming like crazy this morning. Are you feeling better now?" I told her: "black pants, white blouse, green eyes, and short hair." She told me: "Rafael, you are describing how I look today!" I confidently replied: "Yes, I am! Because I was blind, but now I see".

Resistance tells you that your miracle is just around the corner. Its job is to try to discourage you when you are just one step away from your miracle. You will never achieve a remarkable victory without facing opposition. If there is something I am sure of, it is that although I never got to boxing, my life has been a huge fight. The same enemy is the one who sends the resistance to your life, and if there is something that worries him, it is fighting against an opponent who has nothing to lose. In my case, I had lost everything. Out of all the things that I had already lost, what else could I possibly lose? It seemed as if there was nothing left of me, but I was willing to fight for my miracle with the bit of strength that I had left—starting with the miracle of my sight. And after having regained my vision, I was after the miracle of my life. I was determined; that cancer had to go, one way or another. I was no longer willing to allow it to continue stealing my life.

So if you have lost a lot in life and feel at the end of everything you can possibly lose, get ready! Well, your winning season has arrived. If you face resistance in your life, don't let it steal the miracle from you; rather, rejoice. The pressure you feel tells you, "I'm here because your miracle is just around the corner." You're next on God's list for a miracle. You can begin screaming and celebrating because victory has a big mouth. Defeat, on the other hand, cannot be heard because its mouth is too small.

Chapter 19

Don't Let Yourself Die

I could not afford to lose more than what I had already lost. It seemed to me like I had hit rock bottom. Still, I was about to use the same pressure I experienced on my way down to now go up. Whenever you find yourself at your lowest point, you are in a place where it is impossible to sink further down. That realization helped me understand that my time to climb had come.

After many months in hospital, my doctor sent me home for a two-week break. Pastor Glen Harvey, whom I love like a father, reached out to me from Vineland, NJ. Glen often phoned me, but he had yet to visit me since I started my battle with cancer. At the beginning of my struggle, he had relocated from Jersey City to Vineland. Under God's direction, together with his wife, they started a new church two hours away from Newark.

Before his departure, God used me to speak to him about that church and the people that God would deliver into his hands. Even as far as the details of the house and acres of land that God would hand over to him. After that prophecy, I fell ill with cancer, and I did not get to see the realization of that Word. In June 2008, Glen called me and told me that God prompted him to visit me and take me to where he was currently living and pastoring. It was his wish that the congregation would get to know the prophet used by God to foretell what was now known as the House of Restoration, his church. My immediate response was: "Glen, I can't walk anymore, and I don't want you to see me like that. I also have no hair, and I am constantly vomiting. I would feel extremely ashamed if the people witness a prophet with cancer." He replied: "I am your father, and you are my son. If I have to carry you in my arms, I will do so". Those who have met Glen know that he is much bigger than me, and I am no small thing at 6 feet 2 inches.

So, after convincing me, he drove to Newark to pick me up at my house. With only four days left on my hospital break, as I had to return to chemotherapy again on Monday, I began to feel strength when Glen came looking for me. On His face, I could clearly see the sadness of finding me so thin, hairless, and unable to walk. Nevertheless, he imparted so much joy to me. Right away, I jumped into his car, and we took off towards Vineland. Due to my illness, I had not entered a church in a long time.

That day, on a Thursday night, I stepped into a church for the first time since my hospitalization. I immediately began to cry; I missed being in the house of God. As if for the first time, I began to feel life. I felt when the depression caused by my illness stopped operating in me. From the moment I entered that church, I started to feel a peace that I had not experienced for a long time.

I love music, as I have been a musician since the age of six. In particular, I enjoy percussion and even became a trumpet player. As I watched the drums from the last pew, Glen sat behind me and whispered in my ear: "Sunday will be your turn to preach." I quickly answered no: "Glen, I haven't preached for months. I am too weak to preach. Besides, I can't walk." Glen answered me: "Well, it's a good thing that you preach with your mouth and not with your feet." And then he said to me: "Do you want to play drums?" So while his wife, Pastor Michel, prayed to start the service, Glen carried me to the drums. Perhaps you may ask yourself: "And how is he going to play them?" Well, at that moment, my right leg found strength in that drum set. As I followed the pianist, Pastor Michel began singing with her eyes closed; therefore, she was unaware that Glen had helped me to the drums. When she heard the sound of the drums, she opened her eyes. At the sight of me, she began to cry, and all the people present also wept. My tears ran down my face, but also all over that drum set. It was the only offering I could render to God.

Immediately, the mighty presence of God fell upon all those people. I sensed God moving within me, restoring a part of my body that the disease had stolen from me. In 1 Samuel 16, the Bible teaches us about David, a harpist, and how the demons that tormented King Saul would release him every time he played the harp (see 1 Samuel 16:14-23). I made mention of this story because that day, while I worshiped God with that drum set, I experienced something similar. I noticed the disease no longer had a part in me.

Every time I find myself in an altar, I feel unworthy. For this reason, whenever I get the chance to step unto any altar, just as I climb the stairs, I first take three seconds to bow my head and say to God: "Thank you for giving me my life to preach your Word. I am not worthy of such a privilege." Then I shake off my feet and move ahead. I do this in honor of everyone who carried the gospel long before me. This habit is something I picked up when watching wrestling. Most fighters shake their feet before entering the ring. They do this in honor of all those who fought before them. I have great respect, not just for the altar but also for those who carried the gospel long before me and even died for its message. Today I enjoy my freedom, thanks to Jesus and those pioneers.

On this Sunday morning, the Holy Spirit gave me a Word entitled "Don't let yourself die." My Faith was so great that I came to believe that I was about to run around in the middle of my sermon. That God would heal my legs as I preached. I asked Glen not to let me preach in a wheelchair because I knew I was not born to sit there. So behind the pulpit, they placed one of those high chairs for me. I started abdicating that wheelchair. To declare that I would never need it again. Unless you begin to remove the things in your life that keep you sick, you will never see a miracle.

When Bartimaeus shouted, Jesus heard his cry and summoned him. Immediately, all those who recently shouted at him saying, "Shut up," now encouraged him: "Come, the teacher is calling you." Bartimaeus then does something that inspires me. Even before he reaches Jesus, he takes off his cloak (Mark 10:50). In those days, the law obligated every blind man to wear a cloak as a public announcement of their disability. So as Bartimaeus took off his cloak, he declared: "After today, I will never be blind again."

The time has come for you to remove from your life everything that keeps you blind. Jesus was ready to heal Bartimaeus because there was no longer a cloak over him. Living by Faith does not mean that we have to wait for God to do something so that we could respond. Faith involves actions that cause God to do the miracle. Don't look to take off your cape after the miracle. With your Faith, remove everything that defines you as incapable before the miracle occurs. Faith will make you rid yourself of the medicines prescribed by the doctor. Faith will motivate you to dispose of your cane, your wheelchair. And as you release them, they will say to Jesus, "I am ready for my miracle." As I let go of my wheelchair, I said to God, "I am ready to be healthy. I know You will heal me. I am more than sure that You will do it".

As I preached, I declared that this cancer was not the end of me. With every word, I further affirmed that the fact that I had cancer did not take away my role as prophet. Above all, I was able to establish that I had cancer, but cancer did not have me. There are moments in life when we have to fight while God performs the miracle. David had to flee from Saul even after God had promised him the kingdom (1 Samuel 19). If that woman with the issue of blood had not been willing to crawl, she would have died (Luke 8: 43-48). We cannot let ourselves die while God does the miracle. We have to stay active. And if we must crawl, we will, but we will see a miracle in the end. Perhaps today, you feel like you are creeping on the ground, but to you, I declare that this will be the last time you crawl. The same people who have watched you crawl will be the same people who will see you run.

I was bald, without any hair, not because the cancer was winning, but because I was beating it! I will not die without first fighting a good fight against death. Finally, I declared in that message: "The doctors say I have little hope, and the treatments are not helping me. So they have warned me, saying that they will start one more week of chemotherapy after this coming Sunday. Following that treatment, they will perform the last set of tests. If they find nothing has changed in these upcoming exams, they will send me home to die in peace. But today, as a prophet of God, I declare that although at this moment, you may see a Nuni without hair and a Nuni who cannot walk, today you must take plenty of pictures, because when you see me again, you will not recognize me. This is not my last sermon. God is not finished with me."

As you read this, please understand that the next thing that God will do in your life will happen through your actions and the sayings of your mouth because, in your tongue, you have the power of life and death (Proverbs 18:21). You decide if you will live or die. I wholeheartedly believe we are bound to the declarations of our mouths. So if you are going to attach yourself, do so, but let it be only to words of life.

Chapter 20

My Name Is Rafael

After that sermon, I arrived at the hospital feeling motivated about the next round of chemotherapy. So far, I had refused to be photographed during my process, but I began to encourage my family to take photos. I was sure I would soon make it out of this disease, and I needed to show people the evidence. So they began to take pictures and videos documenting the entire process.

On that Monday, when I returned to the hospital, I found the words of my oncologist quite interesting. She asked me if anyone in my family had ever died of cancer. Apparently, I had acquired this type of cancer from a blood relative. Someone had passed it on to me. In other words, I had inherited a curse. The new information bothered me, so when she asked me if anyone in my family had died of cancer, I immediately answered with a no. As far as I knew, all my deceased family members succumbed to the same issues: diabetes, high blood pressure, and heart problems. "No one has ever died of cancer," was my final answer.

Troubled by her question, I spoke with my mother

that afternoon. I shared with her what my oncologist told me. Her face changed. My mother remained silent for several minutes. She then proceeded to say: "My father, Don Felix Padilla, died in 1975 from a cancerous tumor that developed in his brain when I was just 13 years old." I was completely unaware that my grandfather had died of cancer. Knowing this, I now dare say, God chose me to break a generational curse through me. That Monday night, I entered an intense prayer time with the Lord, and for the first time in so many months, I heard the voice of God once again.

While sitting on my bed, receiving chemotherapy, I heard the voice of God asking me: "What is your name?" I replied: "Lord, my name is Nuni!" Then He assured me: "Your name is not Nuni. What is your name?" In tears, I said to Him: "Lord, everyone calls me Nuni, but my birth certificate says Rafael." His following words shook me to the core as He said: "Now I can heal you."

- "That you're going to heal me now? At this very moment?"

- "Yes, because you have grown."

- "Lord, I don't understand why, after such a long time, You would say that to me. After I lost my hair, after death visited me, after losing all my weight... now You will

185

heal me? Even more so, would You saying that You want to heal me after I've lost my ability to walk? Why now?

- "Because you've grown up."

Rafael means 2 things:

1. Jehovah will heal
2. Jehovah has healed

I carried my miracle in my name, but I didn't know it. Under the pride of becoming a father, my dad gave me his name when he said: "Call him Rafael, just like his father! At the time, he didn't know he was prophesying my miracle. God is the Alpha and the Omega. The beginning and the end. For me, this means He is in your past, your present, and your future; in all three time frames simultaneously. Science and even one's own watch prove this truth. Let me explain; let's assume it is 10 pm here in the state of Florida, where I am at the moment. At that same time, approximately 350 miles west, in California, it is 7:00 pm. Now let's cross the Mediterranean Sea to Western Asia; in Israel, it is 5:00 am. Since I already experienced my 7:00 pm on that day, this means that California is now living my past. Israel is living in my tomorrow because their time zone is ahead of ours. So they get to enjoy watching my future sunrise long before I do. While I gaze at the moon, God is in California, Florida, and Israel, all three time zones at the same time. And from Israel, His land, He watches over us and says: "Do not cry about your current crisis, because from where I stand, I do not see disease; I only see a big party."

That is how God operates in prophecy; for prophecies are the revelation of future events from God to humankind. It is what God has lived, but we haven't lived it yet.

"A day is like a thousand years to the Lord,
and a thousand years are like a day."
(2 Peter 3:8, NLT)

God can travel through time. He is capable of transporting Himself a thousand years forward and a thousand years back. This ability allows Him to know the whole truth and speak with certainty. For a liar speaks of things that have never happened, but the one who speaks the truth can do so with confidence, just as God does, since He has already lived it. So when He declared to me: "Now I'm going to heal you," it meant while God was visiting the Nuni of 2008; He also stood beside the Rafael of 2019 as

I wrote this book.

I say all this because, after hearing God say: "Now I'm going to heal you," I raised my hands and made a request. "Lord, if you are going to heal me, visit my grandfather Felix Padilla in 1975 and remove his cancer so that I will not find myself today, in 2008, with it, and my children will not have to fight this deadly disease in their future." After that week of chemotherapy, I left that hospital with strength as I had never had. I even had an appetite and began eating without vomiting. I started asking my mother for all kinds of rich and exquisite dishes that only she knew how to make. After all, no one cooks like Mom. During those days, I craved a barbecue. So I told my mom: "Mom, let's do the type of barbecue that only you do so well, because God told me that I'm already healed."

So my mom ran out and bought all the ingredients for the barbecue: steaks, hot dogs, and hamburgers. I sat at the table of my house, ready to enjoy the meal I craved so badly, when my doorbell suddenly rang. My home consisted of several levels. The living room was on the first floor, the kitchen on the second, and the bedrooms on another floor. My mother went to the living room to see who was ringing the bell. As she attended to the person at the door, I was sitting at my kitchen table, enjoying the foods that I had been unable to eat for so long due to cancer. From there, I could hear the desperation in the person's voice, but I couldn't understand what they were saying to my mother. I could only hear my mother's reaction as she loudly said: "Nuni is upstairs in the kitchen; go upstairs where you can find him." To my surprise, it was a young man from the church we went to when I was a child. It had been a very long time since I last saw this young man. That young man desperately rushed up those stairs because someone had told him that Nuni was in his last days and about to die. But when he finally reached me, I was eating precisely four skewers, two hamburgers, and two hot dogs. Because what doesn't kill you makes you fat! Troubled, he stared at me with a face full of wonder and said, "Nuni, you're eating, and you look good." I said: "yes, I am because cancer is not eating me; I am devouring it."

That night, I had a powerful experience. As my new normal dictated, my mother helped me lay down on my bed. After praying, I fell asleep. I came out dreaming that I was preaching before a massive crowd, and I saw myself walking all over that altar. It was a huge site, and there were thousands of people. I saw myself running and saying: "Nah, I'm not dying, Nah, I'm not dying!" I woke up when I hit the ground hard. Except I didn't find myself on my bedroom floor, I was in the middle of my hallway, more than 20 feet away from my bed. Alone! Troubled, I didn't understand what happened. When I opened my eyes, I watched as my mother and sister Fanny came out of their rooms screaming, running, and wondering what had happened to me. As I looked at my bed, I noticed that the door to my room, the same one my mother had closed before falling asleep, was now open.

Right away, my sister Fanny asked me: "Where are your crutches?" Well, by now, my right leg was already functioning. So, with one leg and crutches, I was moving around without the help of a wheelchair. While the left leg, where the cancer had stopped, appeared to be dead. I answered, "I don't have the crutches." She reacted: "Well, how did you get here without them?" "I don't know. I only remember having been preaching and running when the 'BOOM' came, the plunge. I opened my eyes, and I was here in the middle of the hall". Fanny says to me, "Then, you walked." Please bear in mind that it was virtually impossible to get there, in my condition, without the help of someone or crutches. Think about it, to reach this point, Nuni had to get out of his bed, walk ten steps to the door, open the door, and then take another ten more steps.

My mother urged me: "Come on, we will take you

back to your bed." Full of determination, I declared: "NO! I walked in my dream, so if I walked in my dreams, I will walk again in my reality. After all, if I dreamed it, I lived it". Then my mother asked: Baby, what do you want to do?" My request caught her by surprise: "Mommy, drag me until God heals me." She said: "What?" I continued: "Every time someone asks me; Nuni, how did you get well? I will answer them: DRAGGING MYSELF". One week after that episode, once again, I returned to the hospital to be admitted—only this time it was for a routine examination.

To my surprise, and that of my doctor, I had gained 20 pounds. Amazed, she asked me: "How have you managed so much weight gain in just two weeks?" I said, "Because cancer is not eating me; I am devouring it." After days full of countless intense exams, I had to undergo one more biopsy. We had to wait a few more days until my doctor finally visited me to share the results.

During her visit, I noticed that she came accompanied by many young people who followed her. Everyone kept quiet, and with much curiosity, they took notes of every detail of that oncologist. They were all medical students. By this time, my doctor and I had developed a good relationship. To the extent that she told my mother, she felt like I was her child. She stepped into my room and came over to kiss me on the forehead. I noticed her eyes were teary, and that worried me. So much so that at some point, I even said to God: "Now what?" She looked at me and said in a loud voice: "THE CANCER IS GONE!" Do you remember when I told you in chapter 15 that some people would never get the chance or take the time to read the Bible, but as they observe you, it will be as if they were reading it?

The evangelist, the preacher, the one with the great Faith said to her: "HOW?" Her face was shining with joy as she told me: "These students have been asking me the same question as you all morning, Rafael. How does a young man with type 4 bone cancer heal overnight, and we can't find a single cancer cell in him? Now I will answer them and you too. As I raise my hands to the heavens, I can confidently say with a loud voice: 'BY YOUR STRIPES WE HAVE BEEN HEALED!'"

Chapter 21

God Took Them From the Snake and

Gave Them To Me

Following my doctor's announcement that I was healthy after cancer, I had to undergo many more tests in the next few days. Honestly, they worked hard to figure out what to do with my left leg since this miracle was unexpected. Nevertheless, although my leg was without cancerous cells, it remained paralyzed. The massive tumor still occupied the space previously known as my knee. As the cancer left, the knee, femur, and tibia disappeared along with it. The only movement I had left existed in the ankle and the motion of the foot. The doctors could not explain how I no longer had a femur, knee, or tibia, yet my ankle, foot, and the bones of my feet were unaffected. The movement in my foot baffled them, along with how I never lost the ability to feel them whenever they touched it.

Now, a new team of oncologists and orthopedics arrived to work on my case. Everyone who entered was amazed at the miracle that had occurred. Collectively, they began working towards saving my leg and finding a way where I could walk again. They agreed upon ordering a custom-made metal prosthesis for my left leg, which included a new femur, a new knee, and a new tibia. However, there was still no guarantee of ever walking again. After the established plan, I underwent surgery.

According to the surgeons, the operation was a complete success, so they sent me home with strict orders to remain bedridden. At that moment, I received a call from Camden, NJ. It was an invitation to preach at a youth event. Of course, I started to say no, since I was confined to my bed according to the doctor's orders. But then I heard God's voice telling me, "Go and preach. Preach so that I may complete the miracle."

Can you imagine my mother's face and my family's reaction when I told them I accepted the invitation to preach? Not only was it a concern to get out of my bed to preach, but also the distance of the event was too far. Even so, we made all the best possible arrangements to get there. Imagine the grand entrance of a preacher arriving at an event on crutches. Just picture it, while I no longer used a wheelchair, my family still brought it along just in case the need for it arose. Yet, I had already determined and declared I would never use a wheelchair again; I was not born to sit in one. It is crucial to remember that we cannot conform to every crisis that comes our way, making it our home. Start declaring that your problems are not permanent. Don't make a home of what's supposed to be a hotel stop.

Death managed to persuade man, but it could not do it alone; it recruited the help of the serpent. When Satan took control of the serpent, he managed to convince Eve to eat from the tree that God himself had forbidden them to consume (Genesis 3:4). Then Eve went a step further and shared the fruit with Adam. After they had eaten, God entered the garden in order to do justice. Since there is a great divide between God and sin, man could no longer walk with God. This is the equivalent to a man losing his spiritual legs and his ability to walk with God again. However, within His judgment, God restores man, as He said:

"And the Lord God said to the serpent,
because you have done this, cursed, you will be
more than all the animals, and more than all the beasts of
the field; on your belly you will walk, and dust
you will eat all the days of your life."
(Genesis 3:14, ESV)

This scripture indicates that the snake formerly had legs; he used to walk with them. Since the enemy robbed man of his ability to walk with God in the garden, God took his legs from him so that He could one day restore them to man through Jesus. This new judgment established that now the serpent would crawl and move around using its belly. As I declared this revelation, a great and powerful anointing fell on all the people present.

I began to notice something strange in the way people cried. My family also cried and supernaturally worshiped God. I was utterly unaware that for the last 10 minutes, I had been walking all over that altar without the help of crutches. This time I was not dreaming it; I had stopped dreaming, so I could start living it. My tears ran down my face as I thanked God. I worshiped, giving Him all Glory and Honor for completing the miracle. Setting my sight upon all those people, I said: "God took them from the devil and gave them to me! While I walk, he crawls". That weekend many miracles manifested. The word quickly spread; God had healed Nuni. In a short time, what once was an empty calendar, was now a calendar without space.

I returned home in front of the hospital. When all my neighbors saw me walking near the house, they ran over and hugged me. They cried with me as I told them, "Jesus did it." After that, many of them started accepting Jesus because even though they had never read the Bible, they witnessed in my life the evidence of a God who can lift men out of wheelchairs. That same week, I crossed the street from my house towards the hospital to visit my oncologist. I entered her office, and when I knocked on the door, she said: "How can I help you?" Did you miss it? She didn't recognize me! Just like the world won't recognize you after reading this book. What God will do with you will be supernatural.

My hair had already grown out. My doctor said to me: "The last time I saw you, you were bald and couldn't walk. How is it that you're walking?" I said, "Because God took them from the serpent and gave them to me." With tears, she hugged and kissed me. She took me by the hand and asked me to accompany her. I followed her until I reached the same intensive care floor where I had lived without hope months earlier. We entered a room where some sad young men were standing next to an intubated woman. The doctor told them: "This young man that you see here was once in this exact place. His cancer was terminal. I, myself, told him that he would die. But he told me that he would be healed by the stripes of Jesus. Today he is full of health, and there is nothing more that I can do for your mother. So, he is going to pray for her so that the same one who has healed him heals her."

So I leaned towards that intubated woman and spoke into her ear. I touched her and then left. Weeks later, my doctor called; she invited me to return to her office. Once again, she asked me to follow her, yet this time she led me away from the intensive floor. Instead, she took me to her clinic. Upon entering, I saw a lady walking around looking for a drink from the water fountain. My doctor asked me: "Do you know her?" I answered: "No." She continued explaining: "She's the same lady from the intensive care unit. On the day you prayed for her, she opened her eyes. After removing the tube from her mouth, her first words were: 'Who is Rafael?' Since then, we have performed many tests, and they all say there is no cancer. The prayer you prayed healed her." I replied: "Well, I didn't pray for her. I just lowered myself to her ear and said: 'Rafael is here.'"

Troubled, my oncologist could no longer understand what I was saying. I continued explaining: "For you, Rafael, it doesn't mean much, but for cancer, it does. Rafael means Jehovah will heal, and Jehovah has healed. So my name reminds cancer that where I am, Jesus is, and where Jesus is, there is life. And where there is life, cancer cannot be. Cancer and I cannot coexist in the same room together. Either he goes, or I go".

When I was able to meet that woman who was healed, it became an encounter that marked my life. With tears, she asked: "Is it you?" She told me that while intubated, she observed a beautiful green field. As I approached her, she noticed I was not alone. A man, dressed in white, was walking beside me. When I finally reached her, I said the words: "Rafael is here," and then she woke up. I raised my hands towards the heavens and gave God glory and honor while declaring: "Cancer will regret having messed with me."

Chapter 22

I Limp So That You Can Walk

When I was cleared of cancer, my life changed completely. The differences in the way you view the world after you have passed through death are striking. You tend to appreciate even the smallest of things, just like the sun, moon, and stars. I felt like I had been reborn, and was looking at the world as if for the first time. One afternoon after my clean bill of health, a massive downpour fell. After watching the rain from my window, I ran outside to get wet. My mother kept screaming at me: "You're going to get pneumonia." I replied: "If cancer didn't kill me, pneumonia wouldn't kill me either." I laughed with great joy and happiness as I danced under that beautiful rain. It used to be that every drizzle bothered me. Now, I was amazed at how excited I was to see the rainfall.

I came out of cancer, but I now carried two scars: marks that branded me, the kind I have to wear on my body for a lifetime. One of them is literally on my left leg. These scars are the remnants of all the operations that took place. I was saddened when I witnessed them for the first time. I started to cry as I communicated to my doctor, "I have these marks on my body; they are too big." I was ashamed. It never occurred to me that they would become part of me. I often thought of the miracle, but never the scars it would leave behind. When I saw them, I felt as if my breath was escaping me. Those marks would never allow me to forget the torture of that cancer. But then the Lord taught me that scars are good. They're a constant reminder of how far God has brought you. They teach us that all things meant for evil turned out for our good. They also announce and testify of a pain that once was real but no longer exists.

Remember when I spoke to you in chapter 15 about the wounds of Jesus? We established that Jesus is the Son of God and the Messiah by way of His resurrection. Yet, it was necessary to resurrect within the company of His wounds. When Jesus rose on the third day, He did so with scars on His hands and side. Therefore, those scars were significant, for they proved He was the one who had been crucified.

So much so that Thomas, a disciple of Christ, said after hearing the news that Jesus had risen from the dead: "Until I put my finger on his wounds, I will not believe." When Jesus returns to the disciples, He says to Thomas:

"Put your finger now in my hands; and reach out your hand and put it in my side; and be no longer an unbeliever, but a believer" (John 20: 27, KJV1960). The marks that remained are the evidence that I fought with cancer in my bones and won; I was healed! They made me sad at first, but later I realized they existed for something even more remarkable than to remind me of what God did for me: it was so that the unbeliever could finally believe. Announcing to the world: "God healed me of cancer" does not have the same impact as when I roll up my pants and show my wounds to them, saying: "Jesus healed me from cancer. Start believing." My scars no longer sadden me nor cause me shame; they empower me. Sometimes I even wear shorts in public. There is always someone who will ask me, "What happened to your leg?" And that becomes my open door, the moment where I share the Gospel with them. Therefore, this is nothing to be ashamed of; this is power.

The second mark that I carry is my limp. I escaped cancer, but with a limp. However, it also gives me power. There are days when I limp far more than others. At that point, my condition is more noticeable, but at all times, I limp. There are always those who stop me on my way to ask: "What happened to your leg?" I then seize the moment and preach to them about how this is not shameful; on the contrary, it is power. I remember some time ago when I traveled to Mexico for a preaching engagement. In front of more than 4,000 people, I heard God say to me: "I am going to perform miracles." That night, the first to receive a miracle was a woman in a wheelchair. This woman came to the crusade while fighting cancer. It just so happened that she was at the point where she could no longer get up or take a single step. For over a year, this woman had not walked, and doctors had sent her home to die.

She was invited to the crusade by her nurse, who told her the preacher came from the United States and had been healed from cancer. Yet, the woman insisted that miracles did not exist. She was convinced that preachers often paid people to pretend they were sick, and then act as if they had healed them. The same lady who had spoken such words was the first to be healed that night. God touched her, and she stood in front of over 4,000 people. For the first time in more than a year, she walked. I remember hearing the cry of all those people when they saw her standing. This woman was no stranger. Any of them could bear witness; she was a certified cripple. Well known in her community, everyone now could testify a miracle had occurred.

When the unbelievers noticed her walking, they surrendered their lives to Christ, along with their family members and relatives who accompanied this woman; because unbelievers will believe through miracles. All of a sudden, I heard a woman asking the bishop responsible for the crusade: "How is it that a lame preacher prays for the sick and they are healed, yet he is still lame?" Before the bishop could answer this question, I went ahead and said, "Madam, I limp so you can walk." There are certain glories come at a high price in life. By the way, I am not implying that you need to go through cancer to qualify for God's use in raising the lame. However, I am saying that there are challenges in life that will unleash a special anointing in you. Blessings and favors that are specific to you and come directly from God. God did not allow David to fight a giant so that he could remain a shepherd (1 Samuel 17). The battle you face today carries a reward.

The Bible tells us that Jacob wrestled with the angel of Jehovah (Genesis 32:22-30). In this fight, Jacob refused to let go of that angel and told him: "If you don't bless me, you can't go." Jacob insisted on receiving his blessing that same night. And so it was, he got the blessing, but he had difficulty limping for the rest of his life. In an attempt to make Jacob surrender and release him, the angel touched the socket of his hip and dislodged his femur. But even with all the pain he felt, Jacob would not let him go until he rewarded him with his request. The Word teaches us that although Jacob limped the rest of his life, he did so with a blessing that changed his name to Israel and made him, even to this day, a great nation. Jacob limped for the rest of his life so that Israel could walk in the desert without limping for 40 years. I believe that today, I am lame because I didn't give up, even when I felt that immense pain. Instead, I clung to God more, and that is why I came out with a limp. My limp tells the world: "I fought with God and men, and I won.

I say all this because I have declared that I am limping so that my children will never have to, for this limp is not part of my DNA. I wasn't born a cripple. Neither was I born with cancer. Therefore, cancer is also not in my DNA. And since it is not there, my children will walk, my grandchildren will walk, and my great-great-grandchildren will likewise walk. On the grounds that someone dared to fight alongside God and men so that every curse would be broken, they will never have to limp. If Jesus heals you today, he heals everyone connected to your bloodline. When the blood is healed, your DNA is healed. So please don't be ashamed of your scars; they will speak louder than the words that come out of your mouth. They will tell the world that the devil tried to kill you but failed. The giant who once threatened you has fallen and can never get up again.

Chapter 23

They Are Going To Give It Back To You

The unbelief within the doctors was so great that they suggested that the cancer would return at any time. They claimed that although there was no cancer, they did not want to take the risk of removing the port from my chest, where they easily connected me to chemotherapy. They told me it would return at any moment. And yes, I felt as if that port was in agreement with that medical proclamation. As I preached and traveled, the same port constantly whispered in my ear: "At any moment, the cancer will return." One afternoon, while packing my bags for a Los Angeles, California tour, I watched TBN on my television. This Christian television channel is ranked #1 worldwide.

Pastor Benny Hinn was preaching a sermon on wealth and finances. While he spoke live on television, I packed my bags and paid attention to him. I immediately heard that voice that told me: "At any moment, the cancer will return." Then I stared into the television and said out loud, "If you are truly a prophet of God, prophesy to me now. And don't talk to me about money". Immediately, I witnessed when Pastor Benny Hinn stopped talking, closed his eyes, and then said, "The Lord is talking to me." He then pointed to the TV and continued saying, "You, who is watching me on television, God is telling me to tell you that the cancer you had will never come back." Instantly, I began to cry. I fell to the ground and worshiped God. With my hands raised to the sky, I said: "Thank you, Lord, for You not only healed me, but it will never return."

Unfortunately, not everyone who worked as part of my health team had the faith of my oncologist. Perhaps you have asked yourself, "So what was her name?" or "Where is she today?" In 2011, I held the first event in my hometown: Jesus Heals You, Newark, NJ. During the week of the event, we visited the same hospital from which I was evicted. A group of magazine reporters came to interview my oncologist. She welcomed them with great joy but asked not to document her interview. When they asked her why she did not want to record the interview, she told them: "Because I will be confessing that he was dying, and there was no hope for him. Rafael said: 'By His wounds, we have been healed' and I believed him: Jesus healed him." They went on to tell her how wrong she was for confessing such a thing. She then told them: "Not only was Rafael healed, but Jesus also healed all those on the same floor."

"One after another, Rafael unleashed a phenomenon in the intensive care unit that I manage. What he carries is not only released in his room but also throughout the entire floor. The main problem is that if you print this truth in your magazine or in the press, those who are sick will stop coming to the hospital and will head instead towards the crusades. I wholeheartedly believe that a mighty revival will come to America. And from America, it will reach the world. The kind in which ambulances will begin to take the sick to churches and doctors will lead the sick to crusades because unbelievers believe through miracles. I believe a great awakening is on its way."

In February 2014, my oncologist removed the portal. Her words were: "If it has not returned until now, it will never return." I left the hospital after this gratifying procedure, feeling as if I were a student who graduated from university. Finally, I would no longer have to feel the discomfort of this port on my chest. Several days later, I got back on a plane for what we call Jesus Heals You Tour. The Jesus Heals You Tour is an evangelistic crusade in which I celebrate the miracle of deliverance from cancer through the message of the Cross. In these crusades, we observe the powerful manifestation of God through miracles, and we watch as many souls come to the feet of Jesus. The crusade began in Florida and then went through Colorado, California, and Mexico.

At the end of March, I arrived in Denver, Colorado. I was preaching a message entitled, "What do you want it for?" Some people desire Jesus because they want to be famous. Some want to be rich. Others only want to be healed. But I want Him because I love Him. After all, I can't imagine my life without Him. I want Him so that I can help others experience the kind of relationship that I have enjoyed with him. Throughout my life, my goal was never to be famous. Instead, I aim to see everyone getting to know the same Jesus that I have the pleasure of knowing. While I concluded the "What do you want it for?" message, the crowd was already on its feet. The closing is my favorite part of preaching the Gospel. It is where I release all the best shots that I have left. For most people, this will be what they remember most after it's all over. During the conclusion, you have to release the most significant blows you can give because this is when you will provoke the demonstration of everything you have said. As I made this crucial point, you know, the best moment of the message, just then, I felt when the metal parts of my left leg began to split.

The venue accommodated over 500 people and was packed. When I felt the snap, I understood that the metal prosthesis had broken in my left leg. Thoughts began to race through in my head. But how and why? What an embarrassment! For a moment, such worries attempted to take control. When that happened, it looked as if I was about to fall flat on my face into this huge altar. The crowd ran towards the altar, but not without first noticing my near tumble. The people's alleged account described an invisible person or force that supported me and did not let me fall when I was just about to kiss the ground. Then it straightened me up and sat me down, bearing my weight on my right leg so that I wouldn't hurt myself more than I was already injured. As everyone ran to the altar, the Spirit of God began to flow over all the place. The first thing that happened was that a woman in a wheelchair stood up. Then another woman with an oxygen tank began to breathe on her own. Because it's not Nuni who performs miracles, it's Jesus.

As I witnessed all these miracles, I asked God why He didn't just heal me. There I was; I couldn't get off the ground. I didn't even have enough strength to move. I felt all the metal parts broken within me. And then, God said to me: "How do you want others to eat from what I have placed in you if I do not break you so that I can distribute and then everyone can eat?" At the end of that powerful movement, God told me: "Son, you are going to the hospital because what I have done in you is bigger than you think." Up to now, I had not felt any pain, only the brokenness of the metallic parts. It wasn't until they carried me into the ambulance that I began to feel severe pain.

I could not believe it. Again, I was ashamed. It seems that everyone else gets a miracle, with the exception of the preacher. When I got to the hospital, they admitted me. As you know, my oncologist and my entire team of doctors, those responsible for my health, were in Newark, NJ. What was I going to do now that I was so far away from my home and alone? When the doctor who was about to treat me came in, his words were: "I just spoke to your oncologist in NJ. We both agree. It appears the cancer has come back to you, and for this reason, the metal components have broken." I looked at him straight in the eye, and with absolute authority, I said, "It's a lie of Satan! God told me that cancer would never come back to me!" The doctor stared at me with astonishment upon his face and then smiled. He crossed his arms and said, "No wonder your doctor told me to be careful with what I was going to say to you." She told me: "Rafael has a challenging Faith."

That morning, after doing all the necessary tests to investigate what caused the rupture, the same doctor entered my room at 5:00 a.m. According to the records, the last set of x-rays took place in February, and they documented that everything was fine. So, in their opinion, the only thing that could cause such a thing was that the cancer had returned. But this doctor marched in, turned on the lights in the room, and told me, "What happened to you was something good." Immediately, I was angry and said, "I recently experienced a humiliating moment in front of an audience of over 500 people, and you tell me that the extreme pain I feel and my inability to move my leg is a good thing. Is this all good? No, all this is bad." With tears in my eyes, I expressed these words to that doctor. He put his hands on his head and assured me: "Rafael, this is good; it is good because it proves you are healthy from cancer."

Confused, I looked at him in amazement and said: "How can a broken leg prove that I am healed from cancer? Wouldn't it be the opposite?" His response left me speechless as he told me, "Rafael, in the 30 years that I have been practicing medicine, I have never seen a case like yours. What happened to you proves that you are healthy from cancer because your femur, the bone that cancer had taken, began to grow again and is still growing today. And as it grows, it breaks the metals in the leg. "Then I heard God say to me:" Tell my people that I will give them back everything the devil stole from them."

The time came when the bone stopped growing. After further tests, when the bone no longer evolved, they opened my leg again, but this time to remove the broken metal caused by this growth. They put in me a new knee and a new tibia with a piece of metal that would protect the femur that had grown. And yes, it hurt, and yes, I cried. However, they gave it back to me. So this present pain has entered your existence to announce the breaking of something powerful in your life. Yes, it will hurt! And yes, we will cry during the test. But in the end, we will recover all that has been stolen from us. So stand up and say to your enemy: "Give me back what you have stolen from me. I am not asking you; this is an order. "Take away your children today. Take away your finances today. Take your marriage back today. Take your health back today. Tell him: "It's not yours; it's mine." Jehovah gave them to me. Take ownership of your life today. Take your life back.

Chapter 24

Why Aren't They All Healed?

A short time ago, someone asked me a question. The question was as follows: "In your calling, what has been the most difficult thing you had to face?" Perhaps they expected me to answer - cancer. In my response, I considered the fact that Jesus has the power to heal, and He has given me the gift of praying for the sick and watching them restored to health. He has also provided me wisdom so many people can come to Jesus, for the Bible says that whoever gains lives is wise (Proverbs 11:30). So, the most challenging thing I have faced in this call is the realization that even though I carry a gift for miracles and salvation, not everyone will be healed, and not everyone will be saved. Under duress, a follower of Jesus asked: "Lord, are there few who are saved?" (Luke 13:23). In other words, he challenged Jesus by asking: if you are salvation, why are people not being saved? The answer is simple; because God gave humanity a beautiful gift, known as free will. The power to decide whether to accept Jesus or not.

It is my responsibility to tell the world about Jesus,

but it is up to them to decide whether or not to accept the message. Whenever someone chooses to reject the Word, this beautiful gift of free will becomes a curse. Regarding miracles, there are several factors that we must consider. One of those elements is a lack of faith. Jesus went to a place, and there were very few miracles that day. The narrator explained that Jesus did not do many mighty works due to the unbelief of that country. (Matthew 13:58). The second thing that we must know is whether the healing we are asking for is part of God's will for us. The Bible clearly states that God's will is perfect (Romans 12:2). The book of John establishes another key verse:

"And this is the confidence we have in Him, that if
we ask anything according to His will, He hears us."
(1 John 5:14, KJV)

In other words, not everything we ask God for in prayer is part of His will. But, of course, there are times when we can't give up on what we're asking for until God makes a clear determination. Please understand God does not have the last word, as some may say; He is the only word. So I propose that whenever you pray, you always end your request by saying: "Lord, if it is in Your will." In the Bible, we find the story of a king who succeeded in persuading God to change His mind after hearing Him say: "Put your house in order because you will die and not live" (Isaiah 38:1). Because of his supplication and ability to persuade God, the king was allowed nearly fifteen more years. But those fifteen years became the most miserable years of his life, years in which he wanted to die but could not. Therefore, you can imagine God saying: "When I wanted to take you with me, you cried before me and begged me to leave you. Now can you understand what I was trying to free you from?"

God's will is perfect; we must trust it, no matter what we experience. The problem with this world is that we tend to believe that Jesus is a magical genie trapped in a lamp. If we rub Him the right way, He appears and then responds to any of our three wishes. As a result, whenever we do not receive what we ask for, we quickly rebel against God and even arrive at the conclusion that He does not exist. And yes, some of the things we encounter in life are heartbreaking—like dying children and the many tragedies that can occur. The reality is, I don't have all the answers to why they happen. I can only say that I believe in God's will, and it is perfect.

There was once this young woman I met at an event. She approached me, asking me to speak with her. She told me: "Your testimony is quite impressive, it has deeply moved my heart, and I am so happy for you. But my mother also suffered from cancer, and I prayed and prayed for God to heal her, but it never happened. She died, and a year ago, I had to bury her. Please do not take this wrong; I am glad for your miracle. But can you answer me why God has healed you, but he could not heal her as well? If Jesus clearly has the power to do so."

I told her that I would have liked to know the answer to this question. Well, believe me when I say there are people, including some of the children I visited, who died after I prayed for them. In such times, just like you, I too feel saddened and ask God: "Why, if you have healed me of cancer, don't you do it with them?" Then, for a moment, I reflect and chose to trust that God's will is perfect. Now, having told you this, I answered to that young lady: "I long to see the day when I can enter heaven and meet your mother." She asked me, "Why?" I said to her: "Because the Bible says that the Kingdom of Heaven is only snatched up by the brave (Matthew 11:12). I once saw myself in front of some golden stairs. When I began to climb them, they started shaking, and I was not allowed to enter. Yet, your mother, when facing those same stairs, she snatched them in such a way that she did not let anyone take her out and return her to the earth. So, on that great day, I will ask her: "How did you do it? Because I did not find the courage to conquer them."

We must understand that God not only cures cancer, but also heals broken hearts. Just like He mended the broken heart of this young woman who shared her experience with me. We must be aware that each of us can encounter different miracles. Some people are familiar with the God who heals cancer, and others know the God who heals broken hearts, the God who comforts and brings relief. The miracles may manifest differently, but they are all performed by a single God. It may be that God did not show Himself in the way you asked, but trust that His will for you is perfect. God will always be greater than what we have witnessed thus far. Today, I pray your broken heart can be restored through the words in this chapter. Just like this young woman who received healing from all the questions that tore her heart apart. Just as God also healed me from the pain caused by the many times I could not understand His will.

Chapter 25

I Attained The Benevolence Of God

In 2014, if there was anything I learned about my femur pain, it was that growth ultimately was responsible for the pain I felt. My suffering existed to announce that there was progress. Something bigger developed in me, which caused the breakdown of all that was holding me back. Behind the pain you suffer today, you will find how much you have grown. If you are in a painful situation, dare to celebrate; you are growing! It may seem like you are in the process of being skinned, but an improved version of you is about to be revealed. Your growth will break every barrier that aims to prevent the fulfillment of your purpose. Moses' mother hid him at the time of his birth for fear that Pharaoh would kill him. But he began to outgrow his hiding place, so much so that she could no longer find a place to conceal him (Exodus 2). Likewise, God is enabling your growth so that you can no longer remain hidden. You were born with a purpose to be displayed by heaven, not to be kept in secret.

Without any kind of pain, there can be no growth.

The pain will shape and strengthen you. It's like someone who's working for the first time. At first, they feel a lot of pain in their muscles and bones, but later they discover that their muscles have grown and become something big and powerful. Now they have built such resistance that they can endure even more challenging things. The body can therefore resist more, including disease. The growth that took place in my life was above my expectations. It was bigger than I could imagine. Before experiencing the femur pain that caused me to grow, God had been talking to me for months about a wife. In the beginning, when God started speaking to me about this, I refused to accept His word. Mainly because in 2011, a young lady hurt me when I asked her to marry me. She didn't believe in the dream I'm living today, so she decided not to marry me. She had neither the vision nor the Faith to accept the life I lead today.

In order to live this type of life, you first have to be prepared to lose before you can win. It requires complete surrender. This vocation will cost you time, family, friends, and even finances. Even so, I dare say it was not that this young lady was not a woman of God. The mere fact that she was a child of God did not qualify her to be my wife or much less for this calling. While we all have the right to eat from the same bread (Jesus), you must know that that does not mean everyone who eats will be entitled to come with us on the same boat. Without including women and children, Jesus fed more than five thousand men, but only twelve men were allowed into the boat with Him.

Many people fear the single life because they believe it is a lonely one. Yet, this is not the case. I have discovered that I can't make another person happy without first knowing how to make myself happy. I cannot be of good company to others without first learning to be pleasant to myself. In reality, some live in the company of others but still feel alone. After all, you can never love another person if you do not love and value yourself. As each individual achieves marriage, the two become flesh. The single life is therefore intended to develop an improved version of ourselves that we can proudly offer. It is a time to discover who we really are. Furthermore, it is the perfect season to establish a more intimate relationship with God, so that when the right time comes to join another, we can be united in a pure and sincere love. When you discover these elements, God can trust you with your helpmate.

Let's head back to 2014, a few days before my

incident, when I heard God say, "You're about to meet the woman who will be your wife." You can only imagine my answer. I wasn't excited, not at all. I was afraid of being hurt again. But when God sets things in motion, that becomes part of His perfect and divine plan. God never aims to hurt anyone, that goes against His nature. On the contrary, He will allow it when He has seen something in our future that we still do not know. Something that has Him convinced that it will be good for us.

"For I know the thoughts that I have about you,
says Jehovah, thoughts of peace, and not of evil,
to give you the end you hope for."
(Jeremiah 29:11, RVR1960)

By the end of March, I arrived in Tampa, FL, for the Jesus Heals You Crusade. That Tuesday night, at the beginning of the same week when my femur grew, there was a special atmosphere as I preached in that church. When God unleashed the mighty move of the Holy Spirit, I made an altar call that quickly filled. There was barely room to lay my hands on people and pray for those who came to the altar. Nevertheless, I found a way to move among that audience, as there were too many people. I quickly touched each person and declared the name of Jesus so that the Spirit of God could do the rest.

In the middle of this movement, people cried as I laid my hands upon them. Some fell to the ground, while others fell on those who were already on the ground. That little place suddenly became even smaller. All of a sudden, when I placed my hands on a particular young woman, God spoke to me in an audible voice: "THAT IS YOUR WIFE." I immediately said: "No!" Then I removed my hand without praying for her. I moved in the opposite direction to pray for another person, but God rebuked me: "Go back and put your hands on her. Today, I will begin to form in her the heart of a wife so that she can give you the push you need in your life and ministry." As I drew closer, I tried my best to see her, but there were too many people around. I couldn't even get a glimpse of her appearance. She was crying, and her beautiful long hair covered her face. Without wanting to do so, I leaned close to her ear. After all, what was I supposed to say to this poor girl?... "God told me that you are going to make my wife." Really!?

I had yet to see the color of her eyes or even know her name. But, nevertheless, God set me up on a blind date. So I told her: "Today, God wants to give you something. Are you willing to receive it?" She nodded her head in affirmation. Then I continued, saying: "I am about to make a prayer that you will not understand, but it is God who is in control, not me." Then I said to her: "I declare that if you are the one that God chose for this ministry, right now, He begins to form in you the heart of a suitable helpmate so that you can provide the push that this ministry needs."

When she fell to the ground, I got upset with God. I said to Him: "I don't know her name or what her face looks like." We know that the groom is not supposed to see the bride until he can remove her veil right before the kiss. God kept her hidden behind a veil, because Shaina was reserved for me. He did not want to show me her beautiful and lovely face without first introducing me to her spirit. But I did notice her dress. It was completely different from the dresses the other young ladies wore. After several minutes of being on the floor, when she finally got up, I managed to behold her as she moved through the crowd of people.

I only caught a glimpse of her back as she disappeared into the crowd. I prayed for all who remained, keeping the image of her garments in mind. It was the only way I could identify her later. I immediately started feeling the sudden work of God in my heart. Now I was nervous. What do I do now? Who can I share this experience with? People will think I'm crazy. Who, after all, would try to get a girlfriend by saying, "God told me you will be my wife?" Only a desperate person would say such a thing. After I finished praying for the people, I intended to change my clothes quickly as soon as I got off the altar, since whenever I preach, I tend to sweat profusely. Simply by saying hello into a microphone, I can already feel the beads of sweat running down my forehead.

I tried to change as quickly as possible. I wanted to go out and find the girl in the long black suit that reached down to her feet. Strange thing, when I got off the altar, on my way to the dressing room, I found myself face to face with a beautiful couple. Without knowing who they were, I immediately hugged and kissed them as I said: "Father bless this couple." To my surprise, I later found out they were the parents of this young woman. Eventually, I discovered that they did not know me; they hadn't even heard from me. But in that embrace and that kiss, they felt as if I were their son. Instantly, they felt great love towards me. So even though I changed my clothes and presented myself as quickly as possible, to my blessing, the young woman was gone. I rushed out in search of that elongated black suit, only to find everyone gone.

Confused and nervous, after the service, I was invited to eat with the pastors of that church. At dinner, when I could no longer restrain myself, I confessed to the pastors that I had a strong encounter with one of their young people. I asked them not to share my experience with anyone. To my surprise, the pastor tells me: "I know who you are talking about. Today, at home, I told my wife that Shaina would be a perfect candidate for you and your ministry."

My reaction was, "Who?" He continued: "Shaina, she is the only young woman in my congregation who wears that type of clothing. She lives passionately for God." Shaina... I had never heard this name. I looked up the meaning, and to my surprise, it meant beauty. In Hebrew, it also means God is mercy. God's mercy had selected a beautiful young woman for me, but I still hadn't seen her face. I didn't know what she looked like. So far, I had a name, the clothes, but not a face to accompany them. The pastor's wife found her on social media so that I could view her there. The problem was that in every photo, she had her hand in the middle of her face with a giant "X" painted over it. It was her way of proclaiming freedom as part of a campaign against human sex trafficking. My immediate thought was, "God, you have an excellent sense of humor." However, I still sent a message through her social media network. Of course, I didn't want to tell her: "You're going to be my wife," as I said before, that would make me sound crazy and desperate. In fact, if you wanted to know exactly what my plan was, I didn't have any. God was the only one in control of this situation.

My message was straightforward. In it, I explained that while I prayed for her, I had an experience; therefore, I wanted to be accepted among her friends. To my disbelief, she waited a whole day to respond to me. After she answered my message, we exchanged numbers. Since I could not see her face well, I asked: "How is it that a young woman as beautiful as you has half her face covered in all your photos?" Her reply amazed me as she communicated her passion for watching the victims of sex trafficking, set free. However, she did send me a photo on my cell phone. In amazement, I realized she was lovely and more beautiful than I could ever envision. Imagine the relief I felt. But how could I reveal what God had told me?

Simple... by not revealing anything at all and allowing God to put all things in their place. So before wanting to be her husband, I decided to be her friend. As soon as we spoke on the phone, I felt something unique, extraordinary. It felt like we had known each other for a lifetime.

In our conversation, she inquired about the ministry. It had been only a year and a half since she met Christ, so she didn't know what an evangelist was or what it took to be an evangelist. When I shared the duties of an evangelist and how much travel is involved, she told me that her dream was to travel the world, but she had never been on a plane.

Clearly, I could see the passion she felt for God. It was genuine and unusual. I have known many young people raised in the Gospel, but none of them carried the zeal for God that she commanded. After days of non-stop conversation, I came to Denver, Colorado, and my femur grew. That growth cost me almost four months in bed, learning how to walk again. But Shaina and I spoke daily on the phone and constantly texted each other. With each text and phone call, my love for her grew. Whenever I felt the saddest, God used her to lift my spirits. The only thing I would not share was what God had told me, or at least I thought I hadn't said anything. After spending almost four months in bed, I finally recovered, and God opened doors so that I could move to Florida. Shaina and her parents found me a nice apartment close to them, so they could help care for me until I had fully recovered. Seeing Shaina for the first time was like being in a romantic movie. Even in my crutches, I advanced towards her in slow motion with romantic music playing in the background. Her temperance was unlike anything I've known before in any young woman. Her simplicity captivated me.

I noticed how she carried herself with humility and sustained a passion for protecting what belongs to God. Every day, she made sure I ate and didn't lack anything. Shaina even helped me to walk fully again. On our first dates, she became my human crutch whenever we went out. Experience has shown me that you don't really get to know people's hearts in good times. However, in bad times, everyone around you will indeed reveal their hearts. I noticed Shaina had fallen in love with me, even without regaining my ability to walk well. The fact that I could not walk properly didn't matter to her. Day after day, I began to fall deeper in love with her without revealing the love I felt for her. You ask yourself, "Why not?" Well, I was waiting for the sign I requested from God in 2012. At that time, I said to God: "The day you are ready to give me a wife, send her to me with a red rose in hand. Since girls don't usually give boys flowers, in this, I will know that God sent her for me."

One afternoon, Shaina said to me, "So, we're getting married?" Baffled, I looked at her and said: "What are you talking about?" All of a sudden, she pulled out her phone and showed me the text message I had sent her from the hospital bed, saying: "I long to see the day we get married because God told me that would be my wife." That's right, under the influence of medication, I told her what God shared with me, and I had no memory of it. After all, she never even replied to that text. Until this moment, she had never spoken to me about it. And I said to her: "What do you want from me?" Her words are forever impressed upon my heart and mind. She told me: "I want your God to be my God and your land to be my land. Wherever you go, I want to be right beside you, carrying the message of Jesus Christ to the world. I want to give you the boost you need in your life and your ministry" (Ruth 1:16).

That night, I went into prayer. I said: "God, if this is her, why hasn't she given me the rose I asked for?" The next day, Shaina took me out on a date. At the end of our date, she escorted me to my apartment door with a rose in hand. I couldn't hold back the tears coming from my eyes. I asked her why she gave me a rose, and she told me: "I've been praying for days, and God has relentlessly asked me to buy you a rose. At first, I said no, because girls usually don't give boys flowers." A year later, I proposed to her, and on June 18, 2016, Shaina and I arrived at the altar of God to promise our eternal love. God's blessing was upon our wedding, as He provided us with the wedding of our dreams. From Abraham Veláquez singing at the ceremony to the white horse Cinderella carriage transporting us to the party. Our sponsors, Nimsy López and Micky Mulero, closed the party with Unción Tropical. With all these Christian Latin singers, people tell us to this day that they have never seen a wedding like ours.

Others who are about to marry say they want such a wedding for themselves. I dare say God blessed us, not only because we honor Him with our lives, but also because we placed the first wedding invitation on the altar in the Name of the Father, Son, and Holy Spirit. For us, it would be useless to invite our family and our closest friends if those three beings, whom Shaina and I love more than anything else, were not present. Mainly because, what God joins together; no man on earth can separate. We wanted to celebrate a marriage, rather than merely have a wedding. Weddings last for a few hours, but marriage is for a lifetime. Many work tirelessly until the wedding day to ensure that the details are exactly as they dreamed. They ignore the important responsibility of working on themselves, preventing them from entering marriage with a healthy spirit and mind. Above all things, if God is the center of everything, there is no way to lose.

Days before the wedding, God spoke to me about my life. He told me, "With this union, I give you two audiences you have never had before." The first was the American audience. Since my childhood, I have always preached in my native language, Spanish. Shortly, I received an invitation to the channel TBN Salsa. Their program, Praise The Lord, asked me to preach an entire message in English. In that television show, the supernatural power of God came descended. That night, at the end of the show, the audience testified of the mighty things God did through our participation. God then opened the doors so that I could reach the American people and American churches. As a result, today, I am the host of our own TBN SALSA network television program - (Virtue).

After a few months of marriage, God gave me the second audience. When Shaina and I arrived in Myrtle Beach, South Carolina, the local pastors received us with much love and joy. They told us that people were in great anticipation of miracles. They also reported how sorry they felt for a lady visiting the church for more than a month, who was deaf and dumb. She would come and sit without understanding a single word of what was said. But somehow, every service, there she was, sitting and enjoying without comprehension. I told them: "Today, she will understand." With an amen, they agreed and declared that perhaps God would heal her.

It is essential to take the time to know the people you will connect with in life. Personal connections can determine whether your vision will expedite up or remain stagnant. Some people do not prosper because they stay in wrong relationships. For this reason, we must always consult God in this matter, especially when it comes to a life-altering covenant like marriage. When God favors an association, whether in marriage, friendship, or business, it can only prosper. If you suffer from a lack of prosperity in any relationship, you should know that God is not involved in this union. Simply put, this union can't come from God.

When I initiated my sermon, I took Shaina by the hand and brought her right next to me. As I preached, Shaina started moving her hands. No, she didn't break into a liturgical dance; it was because Shaina is a sign language interpreter for the deaf and dumb. So, we watched this woman cry as she realized the message of Christ was being preached to her through the hands of my wife. Then I noticed the woman answering my wife with her hands, and they originated a conversation. When I asked Shaina what was happening, she replied: "She is accepting Jesus as her Savior."

If the world is incapable of understanding the message that flows out of my mouth, they will appreciate it as they watch my wife. This woman is not the only one who came to Jesus through the message from my wife's hands. Others, just like her, have also made the confession of Faith. Even the deaf will somehow hear this message. We cannot limit God; this Gospel will be preached until everyone hears. Today, we travel together all over the world. When invited, if the four of us are not welcomed, I alone cannot accept. The four of us? Yes, Shaina and I are one flesh, plus the Father, Son, and Holy Spirit.

Shaina is a gift from God to my life. She has such an impressive Faith. Sometimes even more than I do. But then again, I always asked God for a woman with greater Faith than me. Even when it comes to this book you are reading today, I dare say it was her Faith that produced it, because when I denied I was an author, she reminded me of God's promise for my life. Well, I haven't told you anything yet about the woman who arrived at my hospital room in Denver, Colorado, on May 18, 2014. So many people ignored her and believed she was crazy. Then, on my birthday, she came to me to deliver a Word from God.

That woman told me, "God has planted a young woman in your life whom He has chosen to be your wife. And when you leave this place, God will hand her over to you. And after you enter into the covenant of marriage, God will also deliver a book into your hands." Whether she was crazy or not, I do not know, but of this one thing I'm sure: this woman's words came directly from the throne of God. As you can see, today I live traveling the world with Shaina, and here you are reading this book. Shaina is remarkable. Once, she told me that she would have wanted to take care of me during my battle with cancer. I replied: "I have been healed of my cancer, thanks also to your prayers." Baffled, she said to me: "What prayers are you talking about if I didn't know you or who you were?" I then asked: "Did you ever pray to God for your future husband? Tell me, did you ask God to make him just as I am today? Did you ever say to Him: Give me a husband!" As she answered, "yes," I then said: "Well, then your prayer healed me." "But how?" she still questioned. I clarified, "every time you prayed to God for your eventual husband, you actually said to Him: Heal Nuni, because if you do not heal him, he will never become my husband." And well, here I am. And well, here I am. I found the benevolence of God, for the Bible says:

"He who finds a wife finds a good thing,
and he obtains the benevolence of Jehovah."
(Proverbs 18:22, KJV)

Every day Shaina reminds me that God's favor is with me. That, no matter how difficult the road may seem, together we will reach the end. That I don't deserve anything I have, but if I have it, it's because the beautiful mercy of God accompanies us day and night. She is my shield, for God did not extract the woman from the man's back. So I do not believe in the saying, "behind every great man, there is a great woman." Instead, I say next to every great man, there is a great woman of God. The day Shaina arrived, my loneliness packed its bags and left, never to return. I live eternally grateful to God for her. The best armor-bearer a man can have is his wife. Shaina and I live from plane to plane, not because we are tourists, but because we recognize the call God has placed in us. Our house is almost always unoccupied, and the fridge is empty. Simply because we are rarely there, but no matter where Shaina and I may be, we are at home if we are together.

When I was single, people said to me: "You're going to miss the train." I would answer them: "I'd rather have the train leave me than the train running over me." Never let people's comments force you into a season in which God Himself does not ask you to enter. Also, don't get married just because you struggle with sexual impurity; marriage will not solve that problem. Weakness should never be the reason for entering into a life-long commitment. The basis for marriage should always be to become part of a covenant that builds something beautiful before the eyes of God. Marriage is an institution ordained by God in the Garden of Eden. It was the first ministry God gave to man on earth.

Others would say: "Marry a young woman who can sing." Yet, in reality, it was not a singer I needed. I was lacking was a young woman who loved God more than she loved me. Someone with a desire to honor God above all things. Someone who would not even consider denying the name of Jesus in difficult times. I needed a young woman who could understand me, because I am a complicated boy. A young woman who might not prophesy but knows how to pray. Someone who has wholeheartedly devoted their life to prayer, for prayer is the key to a healthy relationship with God. There are days when I sense a supernatural force, and then I realize Shaina is praying for me. So many times while I sleep, I can feel her hand on my forehead as she prays for me.

Many people will describe a person of ministry as one who preaches before crowds, sings in front of a large audience, or someone considered a leader. But Shaina showed me otherwise. During my travels, I have known people who sing and preach worldwide, but are filled with fame instead of prayer. When we pray, wise decisions are made. I live unafraid of what will happen tomorrow, knowing that our marriage is secure because Shaina prays. Her primary ministry is intercession. I do not doubt that a time will come when she will preach with more than her hands. One day God will open her mouth so that she can speak the Word of God. But until that day, we continue to convey the Gospel message through their hands.

Shaina is a warrior. She stands in the gap for us every day in prayer. Without any obligation, she puts herself in my place and bows her knees for both of us. When the enemy arrives, he finds a wall of protection because long before he came, Shaina had prayed. Every day she works on reinforcing that wall. For "the wise woman is the one who builds her house" (Proverbs 14: 1).

If you are in your season of singleness, still waiting for your partner, anxious to know who your husband or wife will be, do not make your choice based on how beautiful they sing or because they have a calling or leadership skills. Instead, make your choice based on how they pray. For life depends on prayer. If you do, I can guarantee you that your partner will always choose God and you over everything, especially when the tough days show up. So before planning a fancy wedding, it is best to focus on God and a successful marriage, for He is at the center of it all. Always remember, the wedding will quickly be over, but the marriage will last forever.

Chapter 26

Divina

During my illness, I heard God telling me, "Preaching alone is not enough." In my mind, I began watching a film full of unhappy children struggling in hospitals with the same illness as me. A few years after leaving the hospital, I was able to launch "Divina: Children Against Cancer," an organization dedicated to bringing joy and smiles to children who are diagnosed with cancer. Divina is an extension of our "Divine Healing" Ministry. In six years, we have brought smiles to over 1,550 children.

Throughout the year, we visit many children in the United States, especially during the Christmas season. I love Christmas mainly because it is when we celebrate Jesus' birthday. Since birthday celebrations are reserved for the living and not the dead, Christmas is also an announcement that Jesus is alive. As we celebrate His birthday, I dedicate myself to bringing even more smiles than we have in the rest of the year. Our team works hard to prepare all kinds of gifts purchased by this servant. Through the year, we plan ahead, setting aside a special fund for these children. Often, we can buy the exact gift they asked for. Sometimes the gift becomes a payment towards medical treatments or helping those struggling to pay the mortgage on their house.

Thank God for those people who will contact us to offer their help, giving children and their families reasons to smile. Divina becomes a bridge for good works. Although many wish to remain anonymous, I have named them Earthly Angels.

While I was suffering through my cancer, I lost my smile. So today, I do this because it is the only true Gospel, and because Jesus said:

"For I was hungry, and you gave Me food;
I was thirsty, and you gave Me drink;
I was a stranger, and you took Me in;
I was naked, and you clothed Me;
I was sick, and you visited Me;
I was in prison, and you came to Me."
(Matthew 25:35-36, NKJV)

I have the feeling that every time I do this, I make Jesus smile. Overall, it is my constant prayer that God would grant me the opportunity to make Him smile. Another reason why I do what I do is because I faithfully believe every smile helps ease the burden. Oftentimes, we tend to live our days constantly complaining about the things we do not have while ignoring one of the most crucial facts of life; we have nothing without health. And if we have health, we've got everything.

As believers, our duty is to live selflessly; that is what the Gospel is all about. Jesus taught and demonstrated the very principle against selfishness. He goes so far as even to encourage us to give our only coat to a neighbor who does not have one. The Gospel is about serving. I find it difficult to understand why so many people fight for positions within the four walls of their church while hospitals offer an abundance of openings. There is a whole world of sick people surrounding us. If they are to find divine healing, we must get off our pulpits and, once again, come in contact with people.

Jesus himself was a Nazarene, which meant He carried a divine assignment. And as such, He carried on with the task of not sharing in the lifestyle of others. One of the special requirements did not allow Him to attend funerals, since He could not be in the same room as a dead man, much less touch one. However, in Luke 7:11-16, we see Jesus stopping a coffin to touch the body of a deceased young man. When He touched the boy, the dead man came back to life, and Jesus brought him back to his mother. For Jesus, the miracle was more important than the title of Nazarene, which He carried.

The same Jesus also said whoever serves is the greatest of all. Jesus did not come into the world to be served, but to serve (Luke 22:27). Unfortunately, there is a misconception about what it means to be a minister. Above all, the definition of "minister" is to be a servant. As ministers and children of God, we must possess the heart and eyes of Jesus, viewing the world with much compassion. We must always be available to live within reach of those most in need. For this reason, after fighting cancer, God moved me to start this beautiful project, Divina.

In the years that Divina has been in operation, many experiences have marked my life. Among the many testimonies that arose from visiting children's hospitals, I will tell you about two specific incidents that have changed my life. First of all, I would like to state that the face of a child battling cancer is priceless. Their smiles are the engine that drives me to provide the finest service. In December 2014, we traveled to Gainesville, Fl. We gained access to visit over 200 children through one girl, providing each child with a beautiful Christmas present. Our team members arrived dressed in Christmas costumes, ready to impart joy; we even had a Santa Claus. When we arrived at the hospital parking lot, we began to prepare the wagons according to the floor order, where we would deliver all those beautiful gifts. Then, while we were getting them ready, I heard God tell me: "First, stop by the intensive care unit and visit all the children who are there." Immediately, I replied, knowing full well that I did not have access to that facility, "No one enters intensive care." I even reminded God that we only had permission to enter the floors where children were in no critical condition.

Please keep in mind that visiting a child fighting cancer is not an easy task. Not only does the hospital impose many restrictions on you, but they are also highly vigilant about who your staff will be and what type of gifts you will bring. For that same reason, we do not accept gift donations. Instead, I, your servant, and my wife purchase every gift. We also train our team to be considerate and respectful of the health of each visited child., including the restrictions on the intensive care unit. Now God is requesting something from me outside the limits, and impossible for me to comply. One more time, I remind God that our permit will only allow us to access the rooms where the children are not in critical condition. He then told me: "Go into intensive care because you hold the key."

So the entire Divina team began to enter the hospital, joyfully greeting every child we met at the entrance or in the hallways. Each kid found on our way received some kind of gift. Can you imagine the faces of all who watched as we emerged with so many gifts? It was even more gratifying to witness the transformation of the sad little faces, as they filled with enthusiasm as soon as they realized Santa Claus came to visit them. Even the adults were thrilled to see him enter. After taking a moment to talk to the person responsible for giving us access to the children's rooms, I said to the volunteers: "Let's go into intensive care first." They answered me in the same way as I replied to God, "We do not have permission to enter." But I insisted: "Come on, I have the key." There are times when they don't understand me, but they follow me anyways.

Upon our arrival, I picked up the phone and called

the nursing director, who is responsible for opening and closing the entrance to the intensive care unit. After introducing myself, he graciously greeted me and said: "Minister, thank you for coming, but you're on the wrong floor. You are supposed to be visiting the levels below. You can't come in here". Then I asserted: "Yes, I am on the right floor. This is where I must start because I have the key". I was worried when he told me, "I'm going to meet you where you are so you can show me the key." As he approached me, I began to pray. "God, I know you've spoken to me, so open the door for us and don't leave us to shame."

The nursing director opened the two large doors. Immediately I felt the cold that came from that floor and the feeling of sadness that lived in that place. From a distance, I could see all the rooms belonging to children in the worst conditions. It was a daunting portrait. I noticed that all male and female nurses were wearing their masks. Then doubt crept in to discourage me: "You are crazy. You won't be able to enter". While shaking my hand, the director asked: "Minister, what key are you talking about?" Lowering my head, I stared into his eyes and said to God: "What key are you talking about?" At that exact moment, I began to feel an intense fire in my left leg. I started rolling up my pants while the nursing director stared at me, quite puzzled. Little by little, as I lifted my pants, all the scars on my left leg revealed themselves. Still, even in his confusion, the director noticed each of my scars running from my hip to ankle. Confidently, I declared: "Here is the key. In 2007, the doctors told my mother that I would die in 6 months from bone cancer evolving from a tumor in my knee. But Jesus healed me. The resurrection account is ineffective if there are no wounds that can support us in telling our story.

That man stared at me in total amazement. His face changed, and his eyes watered. After contemplating the marks on my leg, he looked towards the group of volunteers and then said to me: "Come, follow me." He opened the doors, and together we began to walk through. Part of the stipulation was that I would be the only one allowed to see the children and give them gifts. So while I visited each room, the rest of the team stayed behind at the nurses' desk, choosing the best present for each child. The director also asked me to put on a medical gown, mask, and gloves before entering the rooms. I also had to enter a sterilized room between each child's visit to wash my hands and change into all-new protective gear. Twenty rooms, twenty children, twenty changes. Throughout the twenty times in a row, I did it with much joy and gladness. It took me a whole hour to visit the twenty children on that hospital wing, but we managed to bring joy to each child.

I was more than willing to continue the routine, washing my hands, a new medical gown, new gloves, and a new mask. Especially to offer much more than toys, since each parent received us with great joy on that day, asking me to pray for their children before we left the room. As a result, out of the 20 children we visited, 17 parents contacted us to tell us that the child had improved since that visit.

Then we set out to visit the rest of the children, over 200 of them. While making our rounds, we stopped by a young woman of about 15 years old. This case was particular, since we usually limit our visits to children under 13. Yet, this young lady's mother made a special request that we could not ignore because we all deserve the opportunity to smile. So, we prepared gifts for a 15-year-old girl. Her mother told me that her cancer spread to her stomach. When we entered her room, the young lady was calm. But by the time we reached her bed, she began crying and screaming due to the immense pain she felt. So there she was, on her bed, curled over, twisted, and shouting, "My stomach! My stomach!" Desperately, her mother was searching for a nurse when I asked for a chance to pray for her daughter, and she agreed.

In the middle of her cry, I asked the young lady: "Do you believe in Jesus?" She replied, "Sometimes." Then I said, "Let me pray. Lord Jesus, she sometimes believes in you, but I believe in you all the time. Now, cancer, come out in the name of Jesus!" Instantly, the young woman stopped screaming and questioned me, "Who are you?" I asked: "Why?" She responded, "because the pain went away." That young woman smiled and touched her belly while saying to her mother: "It's gone, the pain is gone." I then answered her question: "My name is Rafael, Jehovah will heal, and Jehovah has healed."

Chapter 27

The Greatest Miracle

In 23 years of ministry, I have witnessed impressive miracles. Miracles that marked my life by drawing a clear line between before and after. Wonders like the woman in Mexico who got up from her wheelchair. Miracles like the young woman from Florida who lost her memory in an accident. She could not recognize her mother, her father, or her sisters. She was full of fear when they brought her to me in front of over a thousand young people. Before all of them, I made a demand: "Spirit of amnesia, get out of her, NOW! IN THE NAME OF JESUS!" Instantly, the glory of God fell upon all those young people. Then, the young lady started dancing and speaking in tongues.

Suddenly, I stopped and ordered her to return to me. When she came before me, I requested the crowd be quiet. I then inquired of her name, and slowly she responded: "Loren." Then I asked what her parents' names were, and she identified them correctly. When I asked for her sister's name, she also got it right. So I moved on to question her about her birth date, which she also knew. Finally, I asked her, "What is your favorite color?", she shouted at me, "BLUE!"

Miracles like that I could never forget. But even so, I will tell you that none of the above will be the greatest of all. Nor would it be if Jesus healed you from cancer, as he did with me. The greatest miracle is when a life surrenders at the feet of Jesus. That's right! The greatest miracle is when you give your life to:

Knight of the Cross, Jesus of Nazareth.

The Son of God.

The Way, the Truth and the Life.

The Lamb of God. The Star of David.

The Cornerstone.

The Expert Physician.

The Light of the world.

Emanuel. YESHUA.

The trouble is that Jesus is often confused with religion, but he is not. However, I must say that religion is not a bad thing, as long as it proclaims the Gospel of Jesus Christ and reveals Him as the Son of God. If it leads to believing in God the Father, God the Son, and God the Holy Spirit. If it stands firm in the truth that there is no other

God beside Him. If it announces Jesus as the only way. And, above all, if it preaches a message of peace and repentance.

The Gospel is the bridge that connects man with Jesus, so that Jesus can reconcile man with God the Father. He is the door to heaven (John 10:9). As mentioned in previous chapters, only through Jesus can we be saved. But in order to be saved, one must first believe in Him. Have Faith in Him. Our works cannot save us, nor can we afford to pay the price of salvation. Jesus has already paid that price for us on the Cross of Calvary. Jesus is grace and mercy, both of which are awarded to undeserving people. For this reason, we called it grace and mercy.

In Luke 18:17, Jesus said anyone who is not like a child would not inherit the kingdom of heaven. The Gospel is as easy as reading this book. I wrote this book in a simplistic way because I want you to know that it is not difficult to understand the Gospel. Jesus demands that we be like children. In other words, that you may have the kind of Faith that they possess. When children play, they use their incredible imagination. Through creativity, they transport to whatever place they want to be. Boys start off in their bedrooms until they open their eyes to find themselves in a castle with a mighty sword at hand, fighting a fierce dragon while commanding orders to a powerful army.

Of course, anyone entering this child's room will quickly realize that he is in his bedroom, right in front of his bed, and not in a castle facing a dragon. He could be fiercely leading the charge with his mother's broom, commanding the brave soldiers to follow him, but then again, when you examine the reality, the boy has neither a sword in his hand nor an army with him. Moreover, he is all alone in his room, even though his Faith tells him otherwise. His Faith assures him that he is far away from that territory. His Faith also informs him that he has reached the castle's door and needs to slay the dragon before entering. This kind of Faith is what Jesus wants you to have. To live in the assurance of the palace that awaits us in heaven. To know that there is a dragon, but Jesus has already overcome it. Just as a child fully believes in Santa Claus, He wants you to believe in Him. But in such a way that no one can persuade you otherwise. God wants you to believe in His Son Jesus with all your heart, so when the evil day comes, the enemy will not have a chance to convince you that God is unreal, simply because He has not manifested in the way that you wish.

One afternoon, a rich young man approached Jesus and asked Him what he must do to be saved (Mark 10: 17-30). Jesus tells him that he must fulfill all the commandments. Also, he should sell everything he owns and give it to the poor. This answer saddened the rich young man. Perhaps he figured that with that money, he could buy his way into salvation. Yet, Jesus is the owner of silver and gold, so what need for money does He have? Jesus is not longing for your riches. He is after your heart. Instead, the rich young man left disappointed with Jesus because He required a change of lifestyle. It would mean giving up things like excessive parties and drunkenness. No matter how much you invest, your money will never buy you a ticket to heaven; you can only gain access by following Christ. That young man wanted to pay a fee for salvation without having to follow Jesus. However, his unwillingness to give up things he considered most valuable led Jesus to make the following statement: "It is easier for a camel to enter the eye of a needle than for a rich man to enter the Kingdom of Heaven." In essence, He stated that it takes a miracle for someone to leave their sinful lifestyle to follow Jesus. Therefore, I say the greatest miracle is not the healing of the body; it is the healing of the soul.

For this reason, John the Baptist declared, "repent and be converted" (Acts 3:19). While you live a lifestyle of sin, you cannot say that you believe in Jesus. If someone really believes, their faith leads them to desire a life that is pleasing to Him. The same Faith in Jesus motivates us to leave everything behind, just to follow Him. Some say only God can judge them. They often make poor decisions and are easily offended when they hear the Word of God preached because they do not want to be confronted. But God has not given us the Gospel to make us feel good. The Gospel is designed to save you, but you must first be confronted for that to happen. Thus, the Gospel will point out everything that prevents the miracle of your soul. Above all other things, the Gospel is good news proclaiming an opportunity to be saved through Jesus Christ. Others say they will decide when they are ready. Question: When will this be? When will you finally accept Jesus and leave everything to follow Him?

My question for those who decide that only God can judge them is: Are you not afraid? Don't you realize that God knows the intentions of the heart? This matter is not about being perfect, for no human could ever be. It's about righteousness. A righteous man is an imperfect being serving a perfect God. "If the righteous one is scarcely saved, where will the ungodly and the sinner appear?" (1 Peter 4:8, NKJV). Others tend to honor God with their mouths: "God knows how I love Him," they say. However, the details of their actions deny their love for Him. A person who loves does not insist on offending the one they claim to love. And while some may insist they love God, yet, they insult Him with their daily lifestyle. It is not enough to honor God with your words. Jesus said: "These people honor me with their lips, but their hearts are far from me" (Matthew 15:8-9, NIV). This scripture implies we cannot serve Jesus by appearance only. We have to live the Gospel in spirit and truth (John 4:23).

On one occasion, I visited a person with cancer who had committed himself to a lifestyle of parties, drunkenness, fornication, and adultery. When I went to pray for this person, God prompted me to ask him why he wanted healing. The person remained quiet. He didn't know what to answer me, so I added: "Why do you want to be healthy? To party again? To continue fornicating? To resume life without Jesus?" I said it before, and I will repeat it again: We cannot desire Jesus solely for the benefits. We can think and care about the health of our bodies, but what do we say about the health of our soul?

A soul without Jesus is sick with sin. So by dying on earth, the soul will be escorted to hell (this is the second death). Perhaps when you encountered the word CANCER on the cover of this book, you may have read it in search of a miracle. So let me now propose this question: Which would you prefer, to be healthy in your body or healed of the soul? If you had to make a decision today, which one would you choose? Let us consider that life on earth is a short moment, but eternity lasts forever. Would you prefer the miracle for the body or the miracle for the soul?

The Bible commands us to stop along the way and ask about the ancient path (Jeremiah 3:16). Today, I urge you to stop. Reflect on your way. Perhaps you need a miracle in your body, but the miracle of the soul is superior to the miracle of the body. And yes, God can heal both the soul and the body. So again, I ask you which one would you choose; a miracle to live in the moment or a miracle to thrive in eternity. God can heal the body, but a day will come when it must die. It is the established natural law of God that men should die only once, and then the judgment comes (Hebrews 9:27). Where do you want your soul to live forever? If you choose the miracle of your soul, I invite you to repeat this prayer today, in Faith:

Lord Jesus, I come before You, recognizing that You are The Son of God, sent to earth to die for my sins. You died, but on the third day, You rose from the dead. Today, I repent of my sins. I renounce all my hidden and shameful transgressions. Cleanse me from all my iniquities. As you wash away my sins with Your blood, may that same blood also heal my soul. Would you please write my name in the Book of Life? May it never be erased. Today, I open the doors of my heart to You, Jesus. Give me Your Holy Spirit to lead me into all truth and righteousness, and teach me to live a life pleasing to You. In the name of Jesus, amen.

If you repeated this prayer with Faith, congratulations! Your soul has been healed. Today's greatest miracle has happened for you. You are now part of the Body of Christ. Now I propose that you find a church that preaches the Gospel. The same Gospel that you have read in this chapter. Get yourself a Bible and ask the Spirit of God to teach you to understand it. Don't lose Faith!

JESUS HEALS YOU....

Chapter 28

I Will Not Die, But I Will Live

"You will not live to see your Birthday" Those were the words of my doctor in December 2007. According to the experts, my capacity to live would not exceed more than six months. But on May 18, 2008, in a hospital fighting cancer, I saw my 23rd birthday. With cancer still, but I managed to see my 23rd birthday. That day served as my inspiration and motivation. I started to believe that if I could see my 23 years, then I could reach 100. By the summer of 2008, I was healed. In September 2008, I was sent home with all the physical evidence that I was healthy. Since then, for me, every birthday has a significant meaning. Much more than my pre-cancer birthdays. At each celebration, I make sure to remind cancer that I am still alive. That God has added yet another candle to my birthday cake. I remind it, "cancer, you failed the day you insisted on killing me."

At first, the doctors said that cancer would return at any moment. But it has been ten years since that cancer died. Instead of killing me, I was the one who exterminated it. Only through Jesus could I do it. The cancer is dead! It no longer exists in my blood nor the blood of my descendants. Cancer took from us my grandfather Don Félix Padilla, but it couldn't take Rafael (Nuni) Cuevas Jr. I was chosen! Selected to finish it, once and for all. To force this disease to give up the power to take one more of those connected to my bloodline. Where others failed, I could succeed. "For I can do all things through Christ who strengthens me" (Philippians 4:13). You, too, will prevail. Likewise, you will win. You have been chosen to destroy the curse, not to carry it.

Many have said to me: "Congratulations on surviving cancer." And I answer them: "I not only survived cancer, Jesus healed me!" When you survive something, there is always the possibility that you will have to face it again in your lifetime. And even if you don't, one of your descendants will have to live through it. And so, history repeats itself. But when Jesus heals you, He reinstates you to your original form, and that disease never returns. Jesus not only heals your affliction, but He also heals your heart. Some survive horrible things in life but are never the same. They constantly exist with their trauma. Some even lose their minds, becoming prisoners, not of the horror that they endured but of the emotional impact that remains on them.

While dining at a restaurant with some ministers, the waitress heard us talking about this book's project. She was an elderly lady. Upon hearing that I was cured of terminal cancer and noticing the scars on my leg, she told me that she had never met someone healed from cancer. Then she asked how long had it been since I was healthy. When I informed her that it was approximately ten years ago, her eyes grew watery. Asking for a hug, within the embrace, she said: "I am not a doctor, but while I held you, I got chills, and I must tell you, if cancer has not returned in ten years, it will never return. Fly high!

We are the experience of God on earth. We exist as open letters for the world to read (2 Corinthians 3: 2-4). No one hears this story and remains speechless. As I walk across the world, some people will say to me: "He fought with God and men and won." But I did not fight against God. I fought along His side; for that reason, I won. Human beings are inclined to fight alone; however, you will not be able to do it in your own strength. You must believe in Jesus. My life is evidence that God is real. That miracles do exist. That for him who believes nothing is impossible (Mark 9:23). Today, my miracle serves against the unbelief of this world. Your miracle will also help others to have faith in the same way. Your testimony will set someone free. If you can free just one person with your story, then it was worth living through the pain.

For many long days, I thought that I would never leave that hospital, that I would never be cured of that cancer. I heard God say that He would heal me, but my eyes showed me otherwise. Yet, despite what I saw, I believed, for we do not walk by sight but by Faith (2 Corinthians 5: 7). I often wanted to sleep during cancer, since in my dreams, I was unable to see my reality. When awake, all I could see was my sickness; however, I appeared in perfect health within my dreams. Whenever I went to sleep, I would dream that I was preaching. When I woke up, I was back in a hospital room receiving chemotherapy. Again I would fall back into sleep dreaming that I was preaching and traveling the world. This excitement lasted until I woke up to find myself in the same room talking to my oncologist, receiving worse news. Again, as soon as I fell asleep again, I began dreaming that I was traveling the world, preaching to thousands of people. I would tell the crowds, "I will not die, but I will live." On that occasion, when I woke up, I was at my desk in front of my computer writing this beautiful book hoping to free someone and celebrate Jesus.

There are days when I refuse to sleep. Finally, my reality has become much better than my dreams. In that hospital, I made a decision. I was determined to believe in God and take my life back. I spoke to cancer, saying: "Enough of stealing what is mine. Give me my smile back! Give me back my health! Give me back my life! I'm not asking you, this is an order". Today I publish this book, for every time the devil told me: "You will not preach again." I launch this work of art for each tear that I cried isolated in that hospital room. I manifest it in writing because of the many times that the doctors told me to accept my reality, that I was not going to live. I spread these pages for those who were waiting for the news of my death. I make these facts known due to the many long weeks of chemotherapy. I publicly communicate these words in view of every night that I woke up vomiting because of the poison entering my veins. I bring this literature to light in consequence of that day when I lost my hair and my eyebrows. I proceed with this composition, considering that I was seated in a wheelchair to be informed that I would never walk again. I publish this book for every moment in which I felt my soul leaving my body, when everything looked blank, while in the distance I heard the voice of my little sister Fanny telling me: "Nuni, stay with me. You can't die yet!"

I want the world to know that Rafael (Nuni) Cuevas Jr is still here. In a world where everyone operates in their own truth, I will live speaking, not of my personal truth, but of the only truth found exclusively in Christ. In this modern culture, no one is ashamed of denoting what they are. Each one speaks according to their perspective, hoping that everyone will listen and accept it. Well, today, I stand firm in the gap, announcing that: "Jesus heals." There is power in the Blood of Christ! God is still in the miracle business.

Many cancer organizations have contacted me. Often with a request to write an article for their pages. However, upon reading that I give to Jesus of Nazareth all the credit for my miracle, they decide not to publish it. Therefore, I also expose this book to them. I will not be silent. Jesus gave me life and life in abundance. If I existed for Him before cancer, now, after cancer, I will live for Him with even more reasons and motivation. The gospel does not lead to shame. This gospel is power to everyone who believes (Romans 1:16).

I laugh hard wherever I go, to the point that you can

hear my laughter even from a mile away. Now I live my life loving with a great deal of passion. I always express it to everyone that I love. If we are talking on the phone, I don't end the conversation without saying, "I love you." I also find myself crying all the time, not out of pain or sadness, but because I know that I'm not supposed to be here. I tend to cry for every achievement of my life since everything I have achieved is thanks to Jesus. Generally, I am criticized for this reasoning. Some do not understand my way of living, yet, after cancer, I feel like I was born again.

On June 18, 2016, seconds before my wedding began, the groomsmen waited at the altar. They sent someone to find me so that we could start the ceremony. As I walked out of the office towards the altar, I returned and ran back into the office. The Evangelist Micky Mulero (Pai) and his wife, a renowned worship leader Nimsy López (Mai), took me in their arms.

Perhaps for just a second, they thought, "Nuni wants to escape his wedding," but it was not like that. I rushed back because I couldn't believe that I was alive and about to marry the girl of my dreams. At that moment, when I saw that beautiful church filled with people and beautiful flowers, somehow I reasoned that I was back in the hospital. That this was just a dream, and at any moment, I was going to wake up in the hospital room. Yet, after feeling the embrace of Micky (Pai) and Nimsy (Mai), I understood that I was not dreaming. I was not sick. I was alive and well. It was then that I exclaimed, "Oh, thank you, God! I'm supposed to be dead! I'm supposed to be dead! Praise God! I'm alive!" That moment was so special that they also cried with me and thanked God as they prayed for me in that office.

I have accepted the fact that not everyone will understand why I live the way I live or why I preach the way I preach. I have come to the following conclusion; It is not up to them to understand; however, I am the one who must understand and always recognize that everything, whatever I have, I have through Jesus. Without Him, on my own, I would never have the ability to achieve my way of life. After all, I don't need people to understand me, I need to be heard. There are special moments like when I am on an altar and the presence of God feels very strong. At times like these the public is devoted to worship; some scream, others run, some jump and even cry. In those moments, I bend my good knee and in tears I thank God for giving me life. There are times that regardless of the audience in front

267

of me, I blow a kiss upward and toward God. In those moments, perhaps the audience cannot hear what comes out of my mouth, as I move the microphone away from my lips. Like what happened at the Roberto Clemente Coliseum in Puerto Rico when, in the midst of those screams, in front of thousands of people, I kissed God and said: "Thank you for giving me life. Thank you for remembering me." I don't deserve what I have. But as long as I live, I will live in gratitude to God, celebrating Him, just as He deserves.

Cancer would have killed me when it had the chance, but it left me alive. So, I go through life without fear. Without worrying about what tomorrow will bring. Because after having survived an episode like cancer, I dare say that nothing I face will be stronger or more frightening. Therefore, I live with my head held high and always giving the Glory to God. I do not exist trying to be accepted by men. Even our beloved Christ was not appreciated by every man. Still, He encourages us by saying: "Blessed are you when you are reproached for my sake" (Matthew 5:11-12). So, I thank even those who at some point did not believe in me. The unbelievers also took part in the publication of this book. Those rejecting you are unaware of this fact; the more they despise you, the more heaven moves in your favor. However, I do not concentrate on those that will not accept me; rather, my focus is on those that will receive me. Just like the young woman who once told me: "When I heard your testimony, I received Faith for my illness, and I too was healed." What matters most is the souls who give their lives to Jesus through your call. It's all about the people inspired to accept a word from God through you. The Lord gave me this life for such people; they are the purpose of my existence. And yes, I confess that there was a time when I cried for lack of acceptance from leaders and folk who thought that they were more important than me. Yet, Jesus, the most important one, accepts us just as we are. If cancer could not disable me, people's rejection will not stop me either.

I do not regret having gone through cancer. If I could turn back the clock before cancer, to a time where God would ask me: Do you want to go through this test? I would say yes to re-living everything that I have endured. Now I understand that when cancer thought it was destroying me, it was making me stronger. I was the one who was eliminating that cancer. As I contemplate all the beautiful things that I am experiencing today, I tell myself: "If I had realized what was truly happening, I would not have cried so much in my illness." But my tears were like rain upon the harvest that I enjoy today and a lens of revelation. God had the power to heal me instantly during my first pains, or He could have healed me from the moment I was diagnosed with cancer. Still, He wanted to show me how much I could bear. He allows it to prove that while He does have the power to calm the storm, whenever He chooses not to silence it, it is because I am learning to live in the midst of it.

Evangelist Billy Graham, known as America's Shepherd and a Pastor to its Presidents, once said, "Someday you will read or hear that Billy Graham is dead. Don't you believe a word of it! I shall be more alive than I am now. I will just have changed my address. I will have gone into the presence of God." The same I say to you today. The day it is said in the news or on social networks that Rafael (Nuni) Cuevas Jr has died, do not believe it! Because I'll be more alive than ever. I long for the day when I can embrace Jesus and kiss Him, saying: "Thank you." I long to stand before Him face to face. But until that day arrives, I leave you with these words: Cancer can't write my story, but it can certainly read it. God has already written it for me, even long before I existed. The Psalmist said:

"Your eyes saw my unformed body;
all the days ordained for me were written
in your book before one of them came to be."
(Psalms 139:16, NIV)

God has authored a book about me, just as He has written one about you. The good news is that they will not end in defeat. We win. A great victory is on its way. If you are reading this book, it is because God ordained it. He established it, and you are going to succeed. This will not be your end. The Bible affirms it: "For those who love Him, all things work together for good" (Romans 8:28). Your troubles will not finish you; you will end your troubles. Those of us who are in Christ should not be worried. After all, cancer or any disease can kill your flesh, but it cannot kill your soul.

In life everything has an end. As for me, this is just the beginning …

"I shall not die, but live,

and declare the works of the Lord."

(Psalms 118:17, NKJV)

COMING UP NEXT:

Hey Cancer! I'm Still Winning!

Battle with
cancer

Chemotherapy

2008

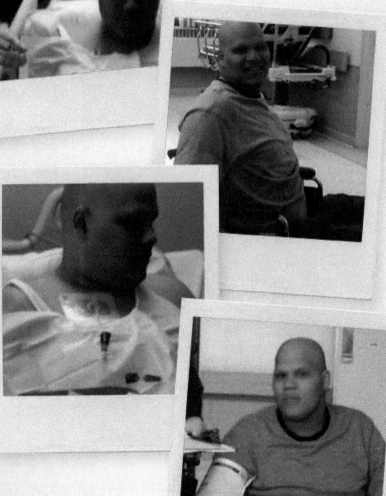

First "Jesus te Sana" 2011
(Newark, NJ)

La Sonda Antigua
(Apostol Wanda Rolón,
Toa Alta, PR) 2015

El Shadai (Anniversary) 2017
(Rochelle, NJ)

"Jesus te Sana" 2012
(Guatemala)

Roberto Clemente
Stadium
(Puerto Rico) 2015

Invited by Micky Mulero
& Nancy López

Wedding
June 18, 2016
Rafael & Shaina Cuevas

Interviewing Pastor Jonathan
Miller on "Virtue" talk show

Interviewing Prophet Antonio
Burroughs on "Virtue" talk show

TBN Salsa "Praise The Lord"
with Pastor ED Ramirez

"Virtue" talk show red carpet

HEY CANCER, I'm still WINNING!

CPSIA information can be obtained
at www.ICGtesting.com
Printed in the USA
LVHW070429300921
699035LV00008B/206